Linking Human Resource Strategy and Practice
An Integrated Framework

Linking Human Resource Strategy and Practice

An Integrated Framework

Stephen M. Flynn

Matador
5 Weir Road
Kibworth Beauchamp
Leicester LE8 0LQ, UK
Tel: 0116 279 2299
Fax: 0116 279 2277
Email: books@troubador.co.uk
Web: www.troubador.co.uk/matador

ISBN 978 1848762 596

British Library Cataloguing in Publication Data.
A catalogue record for this book is available from the British Library.

Typeset in 10pt Tahoma by Troubador Publishing Ltd, Leicester, UK
Printed in the UK by TJ International, Padstow, Cornwall

Matador is an imprint of Troubador Publishing Ltd

Dedicated to the lifeforce of
Catherine Rachel Flynn
1988-2006

Contents

Tables

Preface

For 30 years I have been grappling with the people issues and problems that arise in large organisations. For some 16 years of this tenure, I have been tasked with defining and deploying the Human Resource Strategies for some five diverse businesses. In all that time I have had the pragmatic challenge of tailoring such strategies to the context of each business, whilst bringing my accumulated knowledge (and confusion!) of people management to the party. Throughout, I have, like many HR professionals, struggled to link 'strategy' to 'operational practice' – how to make lofty words relevant to the day-to-day reality of HR advisors, line managers and, ultimately, all employees.

Over these years I have been fortunate enough to have worked for some very tolerant employers. They have allowed me to 'experiment' upon their enterprises and work through some of the struggles mentioned above. Each business had unique challenges and was at a distinct stage of development. Fortunately, each sought a contribution from HR to 'fix' its problems. It is through this very real action research that I have been able to compose this volume. From the solutions that we crafted for the different businesses, and from reviewing what worked and what did not, a generic model started to emerge. This model is captured in this volume.

This book is not just my thoughts and deeds. It is the accumulated experience and ideas of a host of line managers, Directors and HR specialists. The plans and practices that the book outlines, broadly, are the product of some excellent HR teams that I have had the privilege to be part of and, in some cases, the honour to have led. In fact, the 'final product' that is described in this volume arose from a number of HR strategy workshops involving two of the HR teams I have recently managed.

Thus, I have merely captured all of these thoughts in what I hope is a concise and coherent manner. However, all errors remain my own. It is impossible to name all known (and unknown) contributors, yet I should like to acknowledge that a few close colleagues over the last three years have helped me break through the cloud of unknowing to write this book.

Finally, I would like to thank my family, Anne and Dominic, for their patience and tolerance. Their love and devotion spurred me on, even if they may have, on occasions, wondered at the value of me sitting motionless and blank-faced in front of a computer screen. Lastly, my eternal acknowledgement goes to my intellectual inspiration, Catherine Rachel Flynn: a much missed and much loved scholar.

Introduction

Purpose of this Book

Human Resources (HR) is often described as a service function in the world of work. How the function can or should service its client organisation is the subject of many a course, dozens of conferences and hundreds of textbooks. However, as a 'service' function it is in danger of being rendered subservient to other apparently more strategic functions such as production, marketing, sales, etc.

HR is regularly exhorted to take a more strategic approach. Yet, most of the literature on HR strategy is either simplistic or general, emphasising the contingent nature of strategy; or when it gets specific, it lapses into the operational. If we get lost in such operational matters, we default to the jargon of HR. HR technical language rarely seems to match that of 'strategic' or business language. Perhaps this is one of the reasons why HR is often denied a seat on the Board or at the top table.

The purpose of this book is to attempt to bridge the gap between strategy and practice for HR. Specifically, the aims of the book are to offer a framework that:

1.   Integrates HR operational practices with strategy

2.   Is relevant to all organisations at all stages of organisational development

3.   Is a diagnostic tool, and

4.   Provides a template for HR action.

This may appear ambitious. However, the framework offered may act as a basis for others to add to. As this work is born out of experience, others may readily modify it to match their own experience. This volume is very much 'work in progress'.

Structure of the Book

Chapter 1
We offer a core purpose or mission of Human Resources to give focus to the profession and all its activities. Without purpose, any set of actions will be a ragbag of (potentially) irrelevant tasks. We then build on this by describing the six generic pillars of the HR (Strategic) Framework.

Chapter 2
We then set our discussion in the organisational context. We outline the four maturity levels that define the stages of development applicable to any and all organisations. We then develop this into the four complementary HR levels of maturity that match those of the organisational.

The combination of the six pillars of the HR Framework and the four maturity levels gives us the HR Maturity Matrix. This is the backbone of the whole book. The structure of the Matrix enables 'strategic fit' through alignment both horizontally (with organisational maturity and between HR pillars) and vertically (within each HR pillar) (Armstrong, 2003, p.116-121).

Chapters 4-9

In these six chapters, for each of the six pillars of the HR Framework in turn, we describe the detailed HR practices and themes that relate to each of the four maturity levels. A step-change progression will be apparent in the sophistication and relevance of the practices as an organisation shifts from one maturity level to the next.

Chapter 10

In this chapter, we present an overall model of motivation that draws upon the structure of the maturity levels and the detail presented in the previous chapters on the six pillars. We show how certain motivations are available and facilitated by each maturity level and which remain inaccessible. We thus demonstrate the scope for and the limitations of 'psychological contracts'.

Chapter 11

In this final chapter we endeavour to draw together all of the arguments set out in the book. A diagnostic process is outlined and a model for strategic acrion for HR is offered.

How to Use This Book

This is a short guidebook to aid the navigation of Human Resource Strategy and HR operational practice. It is not an academic textbook, nor is it a manual of HR tools and techniques. It has been developed based upon practical experience and business necessity. It is less a 'how to' book and more a 'how we did it' book. An understanding of the broad range of HR skills and tools is assumed. Readers are referred to the standard business school and professional development texts for explanations of the mainstream techniques mentioned in this volume. However, where a practice is offered that is not readily available in other textbooks, it is described in more detail.

This volume may be used in a number of ways. First, it may be taken as merely a descriptive text – how a small number of HR professionals tried to make sense of their immediate, confusing and perplexing worlds. Second, it may be utilised as a means of diagnosing the state of play of any one organisation. Third, it may be applied to any given HR department to see if it is 'in phase' or out of step with its client organisation. Fourth, given all of this, the volume may then be used to craft relevant and congruent HR strategies, plans and practices.

Thus, this book may be suitable for senior HR Managers and HR Directors who want a strategic navigation aid. It may be of use to Managing Directors, CEOs and COOs seeking inspiration from a perhaps surprising source. Lastly, it may suit academics and students as either a case study or as a basis for further research.

CHAPTER 2

The Strategic Framework for Human Resources

Introduction

In this chapter we propose a generic purpose for HR. This will give a clear focus for the rest of the discussion. This purpose will be further elaborated by outlining the six pillars of the HR Framework. We will show that virtually all HR practices can be encapsulated in one or other of these six pillars. This framework is offered as a fundamental model of professional practice and strategic development.

HR Core Purpose

In general, without purpose, action is unfocused, random, traditional and possibly incoherent. Specifically, it is impossible to determine how HR can attempt to contribute to an organisation's well-being without a clear sense of purpose. Further, without such a purpose, it is impossible for staff in the HR function to test what activities they should get involved in and what activities are peripheral or irrelevant to their professional practice.

There have been many attempts to define HR, but the statement of core purpose that we have found most useful and operational is as follows:

➤ *Raising People and Organisational Capability and Performance;*
  – *To facilitate business success.*

➤ *Enhancing Worklife Satisfaction, Significance and Balance;*

The choice of the word 'raising' reflects the fact that there is no end-game but a vector or direction. Strategic development is an ongoing journey. Further, HR is not just the 'people profession' but the 'organisational profession'. We 'manage through organisation' not simply through people (Collins, 2000, p.64-66). Primarily, this is in the context of the large organisation. For practical reasons this is any organisation over (approximately) 150 employees. On average, beyond this limit, it becomes increasingly difficult psychologically to hold all of the implied social relationships in one's head (Barrett et al, 2002, p.245). Hence, as groups get ever larger, the 'personal' is replaced by the 'systematic'. However, people are still at the heart of HR work.

In the HR core purpose, the focus is both short and long-term. There is the immediate performance that must be raised, but also the current capability. Current capability provides the potential for future enhanced performance. In an organisational context this is why we seek to enhance competence – it is an investment in the future.

Overall, the higher purpose – the 'why' of HR – is business success.

HR is not an end in itself. It is firmly in place to contribute to success. Hence if HR cannot readily demonstrate that an activity ultimately adds value to the business, it is, at best, a 'nice to have', and at worst, a costly distraction or an indulgent hobby.

On the other hand, HR is rarely focused purely on the outputs of organisational performance. It also fulfils the role of employee advocate or champion (Ulrich, 1998). The degree to which HR plays this role varies from business to business. If there is a recognised trade union or other collective representation, HR's role as employee advocate may be less. However, HR always plays some part as employee champion. In this HR has to manage the dynamic tension central to the 'employer-employee deal'. That is, the tension between employee performance and employee fulfilment; hence in the purpose statement above, there is also a focus on employee satisfaction, significance and balance. Satisfaction and balance are self-explanatory. Significance refers to the sense of clear purpose that a well-designed role or job has in itself. Further, it is how the job contributes to a higher purpose in the business and in wider society.

This purpose statement thus explicitly reflects the 'two sides of HR'. HR is at the centre of the employer-employee relationship. HR is constantly attempting to balance and rebalance the demands of the employer with the needs of the employee in the employment context. This dilemma (or conflict) is often overlooked in the professional literature. Failure to recognise and acknowledge legitimate employee interest in HR strategy and practice reduces employees to passive, immature agents (Sievers, 1986, p.337). The definitions in this book thus acknowledge the need to balance 'soft HRM' with 'hard HRM' (Armstrong, 2003, p.107) *and* to provide an explicit comprehensive definition of these two sides. With a clear definition, there is some

7

hope of managing what may otherwise remain obscure and elusive.

However, as this is a management book, the practices and techniques described are unashamedly managerial. It is for authors from the critical approach to management to paint the full picture for employees.

The means by which HR fulfils its Core Purpose is through the HR Framework.

The HR Framework

We cannot 'do' HR; we can but 'do' specific HR activities. These tend to fulfil components of the broader HR core purpose. Most will be recognised as sub-specialisms of the broader profession of HR. To some extent any framework is arbitrary. The key question is whether it is useful in practice. The following framework of six pillars has proven of practical value in a number of organisations:

☞ Organisational Effectiveness (OE)

☞ Calibre & Talent (C&T)

☞ Employee Engagement (EE)

☞ Performance Management Systems (PMS)

☞ Rewards & Recognition (R&R)

☞ Employee Development (ED)

Each of these in turn has a specific definition to give greater focus and clarity. However, all are inter-related and do not sit in isolation of each other. Each informs the others and is in turn informed by the other pillars of the HR Framework. To reflect the 'two sides of HR', in each of the descriptions we offer below, there is an explicit employer (or management) definition and an employee aim under each pillar.

Organisational Effectiveness

OE is defined as:

> Creating Roles, Structures, Processes and Practices; and

> Managing the Processes of Change;
>   – To enable core business processes, and
>   – To deploy business strategy.

> Building and Maintaining Employee Role Clarity and Job Significance

This is recognisable as the organisational design and development (OD) element of HR. OD is central to 'managing through organisation' (Collins, 2000, p.64-66). In large organisations, the structure is in itself a vehicle for deploying the strategy.

The general tenet is: 'structure follows process follows strategy'. Given the business strategy, the core business processes can be defined. Given the core processes, tasks and activities must be carried out to enact these processes. These tasks are then clustered into roles, which are in turn clustered into groups or departments. These departments then inter-relate and have to be coordinated in order to enact the core processes and ultimately fulfil the strategy. All of this is in general OD and specifically organisational structure.

9

In a static world, initial design may suffice. Few of us though feel that we live in a static world: change is a constant. OE itself implies the need for constant review and change in order to maintain and enhance effectiveness. How the processes of change are handled is a loud signal to employees as to what the organisation thinks of its people. It is a critical demonstration of the culture of the organisation. As change pervades all aspects of an organisation, OE cuts across all the other pillars of the HR Framework. It is not so much a specialism in itself, but a core competency for the HR function as a whole.

Through effective job and organisational design, the employee progressively gains role clarity and job significance. The employee can thus contribute to the greater purpose of the organisation and understand where he or she fits. The 'other side' of change management will be covered under EE, in terms of employee voice and participation.

Calibre & Talent

C&T is defined as:

➣ *Attracting and retaining the workforce; and*

➣ *Creating a Critical Mass of Performance Enablers and Change Agents;*
   – To deliver business plans and results.

➣ *Offering Employee Career Opportunities and Progression.*

Organisations only exist if they are populated with people; people of the right calibre. Sourcing and recruiting those people are core competencies for HR.

Given the roles and structure defined in OE, the profile of the workforce can be specified. This workforce needs to be attracted and engaged by the business. This is the whole process of employee resourcing and retention.

Within this total population there is then 'talent'. Talent can be described as the human capital that is 'the difference that makes the difference'. It is talent that will help the organisation fulfil its purpose and achieve its strategy. The specific category of talent that a business seeks may vary from 'performance enablers' and 'change agents' as outlined above. However, these categories have been found to be important for a good number of organisations.

It is unlikely that all employees need to meet this 'talent' standard. An organisation 'full of the talents' could generate problems of its own. Thus, it is not all employees who have to meet these criteria, but a critical mass of talent that is required. Ultimately the strategy specifies what constitutes a critical mass in the unique context and circumstances of any given organisation.

As we will see, actions taken under this pillar progressively enable employees to develop their careers and grow in the organisation.

Employee Engagement

EE is scoped as:

> *Generating 'Share of Mind' for Business Messages;*
> *– To inform, influence and align mutual opinions and behaviours.*

> *Enabling Employee Voice; and*

> *Building Employee Involvement and Participation.*

Communications is set in a context of an increasingly crowded media world. Any organisation is competing with multiple channels of communications, many of which may be more attractive to employees than business messages. However, it is important for the business to get its message across to its own employees and gain some share of their minds.

Communication consists of two basic forms: 'send' and 'receive'. 'Send' is concerned with transmitting, explaining and convincing employees of the business situation and business imperatives. 'Receive' entails tapping into the thoughts, feelings and opinions of employees: generically this is 'employee voice'. If employees do not have channels to air their concerns, grievances or opinions, it will be difficult to engage employees and engender discretionary effort.

Involvement & Participation entails the degree to which employees have the discretion and freedom to shape their own roles and influence local and organisational decisions. In some organisations, this will involve trade unions, in which case we enter the traditional terrain of employee relations. The extent to which an organisation involves its employees in the decision-making process will have an influence on business performance. Those who are disaffected from the organisation are unlikely to give of their best. The environment people work in and the relationships they have with each other and with their managers are in themselves motivators and key drivers of performance.

Performance Management Systems

The purpose of PMS is:

> *Deploying Business Strategy and Aligning Personal Performance.*
> *– To achieve the desired results*

> *Creating an Environment in which each Employee can Succeed.*

This has been the aim of all managers and entrepreneurs down the ages. It encompasses the multitude of systems, processes and practices designed to encourage employees to do the owners' bidding, without direct and constant supervision.

The definition above begs the question over business strategy. The strategy may not be clearly articulated in some organisations. Without some 'plan' it will be difficult to align behaviours other than by direct supervision. Even then, supervisors may still not be clear which behaviours they are meant to encourage, nor may they be clear how behaviours contribute to the greater whole. However, a strategy does not have to be written and explicit, that is 'deliberate'; it may be 'emergent' (Mintzberg, 1989, p.29-34). That is, it may consist of the accumulation of the collective actions of all organisational players as they interact with their environments.

Under this pillar, employees wish to succeed. The extent to which they are able to do so will become apparent as we explore the development of the techniques in this pillar of HR.

Rewards & Recognition

The description of R&R is:

➤ *Creating the 'Message in the Money';*

➤ *Being Competitive in the Chosen Market(s);*
   – To align motivation with strategic intent.

➤ *Maintaining a 'Good' Standard of Living;*

➤ *Attaining 'Just' Recognition and Desserts.*

Money is the consideration in the employee contract. Reward packages are one of the messages that an organisation sends to each of its employees. This will send a (positive or negative) motivational message to each individual. Whether this message aligns with the strategic intent is dependant upon the actual reward practices the organisation engages in. The organisation also seeks to attract employees to join and remain with it through being competitive in its chosen labour market(s). Failure to do so may undermine other pillars of the HR Framework, e.g. uncompetitive packages may fail to attract the right calibre to staff the organisation.

Employees seek a living wage and a sufficient standard of living for themselves and their dependents. Further, they seek just treatment in terms of rewards and recognition in general. We will see later how employees may or may not fulfil these ambitions.

Employee Development

The scope of ED is:

➤ *Raising People Capability in terms of knowledge, skills and process abilities.*

➤ *Establishing Personal Competence; and*

➤ *Developing Performance Excellence.*

Knowledge and skills are fairly self-explanatory. Process abilities cover the individual's capacity to sequence or order work correctly (Curtis et al, 2002, p.514).

ED is not just training, but it may in many contexts be mainly that. A range of techniques is available through delivering programmes, events, processes, tools and techniques. The choice is up to the business.

There are two levels of capability. There is personal competence that must be met in any specific role. These are the basics in terms of knowledge, skills and process abilities. If nothing else, these cover safety requirements and the basic operational practices of the role. Mostly, this is the level of performance required after the incumbent has 'settled into' the role. Then there is the stretch standard of excellence. The two levels represent: development *for* the role; and then development *of* the role.

Summary

We have defined the core purpose of HR and the six pillars of the HR Framework. In our professional work, we have found that these generic definitions apply to many businesses. It is our belief that they apply to most if not all organisations. Within this framework the vast majority of HR practices and activities can be placed at both the operational and the strategic levels. Which practices are most relevant depends upon the maturity level of any given organisation at any given time. A practice has to exist in a specific organisational context. The generic contexts are set out in the next chapter, which explains the four possible maturity levels of an organisation and the commensurate HR maturity levels.

Organisational and Human Resource Maturity Levels

Introduction

In this chapter we describe the four levels of maturity that generically define the stage of evolution that an organisation may find itself. We explore the nature of maturity levels and how any organisation may move up or down the levels. We then match each to its commensurate HR maturity level. Finally we integrate the organisational maturity levels and the HR Framework set out in chapter 2 to create the underlying model for this book – the HR Maturity Matrix.

The Four Levels of Organisational Maturity

In its history, any organisation may find itself in one of four levels of maturity. A maturity level is a stage of capability that is an evolutionary plateau on an organisational improvement path (Curtis et al, 2002, p.512). Curtis et al describe five such levels. Kearns on the other hand specifies seven levels (Kearns, 2010). However, for our practical purposes in navigating HR strategy and practice, we have only found there to be four (so far).

The four distinct levels are:

1.   Compliance Management

2.   Process Management

3.   Capability Management

4.   Strategic Management.

We will now describe the generic nature of an organisation at each of these levels in some detail.

Level 1: Compliance Management

At this level the organisation is merely compliant, both externally and internally. Externally, it complies with the minimal requirements of stakeholders, including regulatory authorities. It does not consider (consciously or unconsciously) any need to 'go beyond' such (legal) conformance. Internally, employees comply with internal authority where absolutely necessary. Where internal surveillance, in all its forms, is poor or absent, employees and managers 'get by' or 'get away with it'.

Business processes vary widely across the organisation. There are no common or consistent standards as such. Only the barest of internal audit requirements are maintained, primarily of a financial nature. These internal controls are those that assure the integrity of data and measurement, for example, financial audits and cash control systems (Simons, 1994, p.84-85). The variability in practice not only applies across the business but also to the same business process over time. People may do the same work in a different way but also the same person may do the same work differently from day to day.

Management is essentially autocratic and adopts an aggressive and sometimes a paternalistic style. 'Good' managers are 'heroic' managers. In fact, little appears to be achieved but through exceptional effort and individuals (Curtis et al, 2002, p.8-9). Crisis management is actually valued (Kearns, 2010, p.101). Decisions are made based upon 'gut feel' with minimal consideration of data or facts (p.111). As processes are inconsistent, and systems tend also to be minimal, there tend to be few 'facts' to hand anyway. As little is known of the 'track record' of processes, there is little information to base decisions on.

Managers at this level tend to define 'management' as producing results rather than producing people who produce results (Curtis et al, 2002, p.18). HRM is thus deemed 'administrivia' so managers frequently displace responsibility for people management to HR (p.19).

The configuration of the business lacks any 'organising principle'. The structure is inconsistent across the business or archaic. It may simply have been inherited or allowed to 'evolve' over time with no apparent rhyme or reason. Acquired businesses may retain their own structures and systems for many years. The structure may have evolved in accordance with the whims of the heroic managers.

The organisation is characterised by a sense of 'irresponsible autonomy' (Ackroyd and Thompson, 1999). As controls are minimal or absent, internal agents have a significant degree of freedom to do as they see fit. However, as there is little sense of a common purpose, this autonomy is effectively misused or abused, despite the apparent good intentions of the participants.

Level 2: Process Management

Under 'Process Management' virtually all work in the business is captured through process mapping. These process maps describe all the key steps in the work practices of the organisation. These are then transformed into detailed Standard Operating Procedures (SOP) to guide the execution of that work. These SOP are adhered to and there is a sense of 'process discipline'. Where a SOP needs amending there is also a change process to accommodate and achieve this in a disciplined manner for the relevant area of work. These SOP are captured in one or more Policy and Procedure Manuals (P&P), or their electronic equivalent. The P&P sets out the individual policy statements, guidelines to managers, detailed procedural steps, related authority levels and any relevant documentation or forms. There is hence an air of bureaucracy that is characteristic of this maturity level. This aspect of tight control is in stark contrast to maturity level 1. At maturity level 2 the organisation concentrates upon fixing the basic work practices especially at the unit level (Curtis, 2005, p.20). Unit level is defined as a department (for instance) responsible to a manager for delivering a set of performance objectives through its own collective action (p.66). Sophisticated company-wide initiatives do not tend to be successful until the unit level is sorted out (p.21). The regularity of people practices helps build consistency and set expectations, which was sadly lacking at level 1 (p.21). Once practices are established at unit level throughout the organisation, the business can then move to developing consistency across units.

Competent Management Teams are present. Management processes are disciplined and efficient. Decisions are essentially goal-oriented. Managers know what the ends should look like and base their judgements upon the endeavour to hit such specified targets.

The structure is functional in nature. There is a clear 'organising principle' based upon skill-set or profession. The organisation is very formal and bureaucratic, even rigidly so (Kearns, 2010, p.101). Jobs are very clearly defined, and are narrow in 'scope'. Jobs thus have clear 'boundaries'.

Employees are 'competent' operators. They know what their job is and they stick to these job functions with a clear sense of discipline in accordance with the SOP. They 'work to standard'.

Level 3: Capability Management

Management adopt the extensive use of 'toolkits', e.g. Total Quality Management, Lean Manufacturing, Six Sigma, etc. These guide a manifest culture of 'Continuous Improvement'. The functional business has defined the competencies it seeks to demonstrate and it regularly enhances the skills and capabilities of its systems, processes and people. Whilst techniques, such as Six Sigma, may be used at all maturity levels, it is only at level three and above that they are best enabled (Curtis et al, 2002, p.25). These techniques all feed a company-wide developmental approach through a methodical project management system.

Management adopts a more participative style and decision making is data-driven. Risk-taking is now encouraged as it is based upon fact not gut-feel.

The organisational structure has clearly defined and distinct accountabilities, not just across functions, but also at the different hierarchical levels. The next hierarchical level up does not merely supervise the lower level but adds value in a different way. Hence the structure is able to become 'flat'. Roles are clearly aligned with purpose so each role knows how it contributes to the 'greater whole'. Jobs have developed into roles through defined but expanding competencies. The structure is further enhanced by adopting temporary and permanent liaison devices to manage the 'white space' between functions (Rummler and Branche, 1995). As no structure resolves all coordination issues, these liaison mechanisms are put in place to deal with the residual problems of 'organising'.

The organisation may still be functional in structure but clear coordination between functions is well governed by Service Level Agreements (SLA). These specify the service standards and expectations of internal 'customer-supplier' arrangements.

Employees are now organised in competent teams. Not only are individual skills developed but now operating teams emerge as an organising principle in their own right.

Level 4: Strategic Management

The organisation is now fully guided by an integrated strategy. In some cases the strategy may aim to develop or change the culture of the organisation. In such cases 'Culture Management' is a more apt title for this level.

Discretionary effort is engaged at this maturity level. 'Hearts and minds' are won over and a 'High Performance Culture' is manifest. The external environment is continuously screened, scanned and monitored for signs of discontinuities. Thus the business is constantly alert to the need for change. Consequently, the business has evolved into an 'open system'.

Management adopts an empowering leadership style and a form of collegiate involvement is apparent. The integrated strategy guides decision making at all levels and thus management has moved towards systemic decision-making.

The organisation adopts a flexible structure. We call this a 'bamboo structure'. In territories that suffer from hurricanes, scaffolding may be constructed of bamboo. This is strong enough to function as scaffolding but flexible enough to withstand high winds. Thus no one organisational structure predominates and the organisation adapts to suit the medium-term requirements for coordination. A matrix structure may thus emerge, but this is merely a transitional form rather than a permanent organising principle in itself.

Employees form Self-Managed Teams (SMT). They demonstrate, as does the whole organisation, 'responsible autonomy'. As a sense of common purpose pervades the organisation, delegation shifts to the (lowest) relevant hierarchical level in the organisation. Adaptation is thus timely rather than delayed.

The Nature of Maturity Levels

Each maturity level is both a static description of a state and also a dynamic description of movement. For instance, a given organisation may be best described as being at maturity level one (Compliance Management). All of the descriptors for that level apply to the organisation. However, some actions on the part of organisational players may relate to maturity level two (Process Management). In such a case, the organisation is (consciously or unconsciously) 'working towards' level two. A dynamic tension would then inculcate the organisation. However, the levels form building blocks in themselves. If level one and two are not solidly in place, level three cannot be successfully attained or maintained.

As a rule, it is not sustainable for an organisation to have activities at more than two (adjacent) maturity levels. An organisation may be working from level one to two, but activities that may be more relevant at say level four will not be supportable. Metaphorically, if the ground has not been cleared and the foundations have not been built then higher levels cannot be installed. In fact, to launch activities that are well beyond the current maturity level of the business will be poor use of resource, time and effort. The energy to maintain such activities will be out of proportion to the benefit as the internal environment will not be supportive of such actions. Even bright ideas may fall on stony ground. Ideas have to find their time and place.

There is no guarantee that an organisation will 'progress' from level one through to level four in a historically linear manner. The actual maturity level will depend upon environmental factors, the nature and character of leadership groups and employee groups and the pressure that organisational players and stakeholders face from time to time.

Further, to achieve and sustain a 'higher' maturity level costs time and resource. As each higher level requires the maintenance of relevant lower level processes, practices and techniques, it is progressively harder and more costly to move through the levels. An organisation may simply not have the resource to 'move on'. In fact, if a business falls on hard times, it may have to retrench and move (or collapse) to a lower, more affordable and sustainable, maturity level. However, as will become apparent in the descriptions of the levels, this may have long term consequences for the organisation's survival and growth.

The distinction between conscious and unconscious action also explains how an organisation may 'slip back' to a lower maturity level. If the endeavour to move up the maturity levels does not remain a conscious intent of a critical mass of change agents within the organisation, then processes may slacken, application then falls away. Descriptors of a lower maturity level may then become more apparent and relevant. Thus, if a key driver for change leaves the organisation, the intent may be lost. If a sudden financial crisis hits the business, behaviours belonging to a 'lower' maturity level may become manifest or even expedient and those behaviours associated with the higher level disappear.

Organisations sometimes convince themselves that they are operating at a higher level of maturity than is truly the case. The apparent presence of a practice or process is cited as evidence of a given maturity level. However, this is self-deceptive. There are five quality levels of 'evidence'. Only the fifth level is proof of the attainment of a given practice and consequently of a given maturity level (see Table 1).

As can be seen from these levels of evidence, the standard demanded to qualify for a higher maturity level will be significant. Low levels of evidence are at best evidence of 'working towards'.

This also explains how organisations can appear to have reached a higher level of maturity but in a spurious manner. For instance, a business may adopt a mission statement, which, as we will see, appears to place the business at maturity level 4. However, if this mission does not pervade the organisational practices and habits then it is at best a fantasy document. This would especially be the case if all other indicators suggested that the business in fact was operating at maturity level 1 – well out of the reach of practices in level 4.

Table 1 Maturity Levels

Level of Evidence	Nature of Evidence
1	The practice is absent. There is no evidence of the practice or factor.
2	There is only documentary evidence of the practice. However, this is a fantasy document (Perrow, 1999, p.373-378). There is no actual practice in use.
3	Practice is ritual in nature. Those carrying out the practice have no understanding of the purpose or rationale of the practice. They are simply 'going through the motions'. There is a 'tick box' approach to the practice.
4	The practice is evident in most parts of the organisation. It is regularly carried out at suitable intervals. Those carrying out the activity demonstrate competence.
5	The practice is fully integrated into the regular routines of the whole of the workforce and management. 'Mind, body and soul' are aligned to the practice. The practice is 'in the DNA' of the organisation. The philosophy and rationale are fully understood and can be readily articulated by those carrying out the practice.

HR Maturity Levels

For each organisational maturity level, there is a commensurate HR maturity level. Just as we offer four generic descriptions of the organisation, we can outline four corresponding descriptions of HR. The detail of these levels we will leave to the next six chapters. Here we set out the four HR maturity levels in general terms.

HR level 1 is designated 'Initial'. Here the HR function is basic or even absent. HR activities exist, but may even be carried out by staff other than HR professionals. There are few concrete HR processes to speak of and HR concentrates on legal and internal compliance in common with the rest of the organisation.

HR level 2 is called 'Foundation'. As with the wider organisation, there are now clear and well-defined HR processes and procedures. There is a strong sense of discipline towards and adherence to these processes. HR activities tend to be event-driven at this stage. This level is entitled 'Foundation' because it sets up all the practices that underpin the more sophisticated ones that make subsequent and higher levels possible.

'HR Agenda' is how we describe HR at level 3. This is strongly competency-based. In common with the rest of the organisation at this level, HR is focused on Continuous Improvement. HR has evolved into a regular activity for management, on a daily basis. HR is in the DNA of the organisation.

At level 4, HR has and is part of an integrated corporate strategy. HR is 'in the line' and strategic in nature. The strategy is no longer functionally HR but a comprehensive 'Integrated People Strategy'.

HR Maturity Matrix

We can now sketch out the HR Maturity Matrix. By integrating the HR Framework (see chapter 2) with the organisational maturity levels, we can outline the territory that allows us to navigate strategy and practice. This is portrayed diagrammatically in Table 2.

Later chapters are devoted to 'filling in' the details of each of the 24 cells of this matrix by describing the HR practices, activities and processes that generally arise at each maturity level under each pillar of the HR

Table 2 HR Maturity Matrix

Maturity Level		OE	C&T	EE	PMS	EM	ED
Organisational	*HR*						
Compliance Management	Initial						
Process Management	Foundation						
Capability Management	HR Agenda						
Strategic Management	Integrated People Strategy						

Framework. As the reader progressively reads the next six chapters, she will notice not only how the HR practices build up under each pillar, but also how practices at the same maturity level complement each other across the pillars. Thus the HR Maturity Matrix shows how otherwise disparate HR practices relate to each other in a strategic context, e.g. how recruitment activities relate to performance management systems; how engagement relates to rewards; etc.

Summary

In this chapter we have defined the four levels of organisational maturity identifiable in any and every organisation. We have also described the nature of maturity levels and how an organisation can only truly sit at one level at any period of time. To match each organisational level we also described the commensurate HR maturity level.

By then combining the HR Framework (see chapter 2) and the Maturity Levels we were able to scope the HR Maturity Matrix which is the fundamental model underpinning this whole book.

The four maturity levels are summarised in Table 3.

The progression from level one through to level four: from Compliance to Strategic Management; each is a distinct step rather than a gradual evolution. Just as changing physical state from, say, solid to liquid requires extra energy, so effort is required to move fully from one maturity level to another. Otherwise an organisation will, all other things being equal, become locked into one maturity level for a long time. The following chapters will explore how Human Resources may apply activity and energy at each of the maturity levels.

Table 3

	Organisational Maturity Level	Description	HR Maturity Level
1	Compliance Management	Minimal External and Internal Compliance Wide variety of inconsistent practices Autocratic or Paternalistic Style 'Heroic' Management 'Gut-feel' decision-making Unclear, inherited, archaic structure 'Irresponsible Autonomy'	Initial
2	Process Management	Process discipline and adherence Process Mapping Standard Operating Procedures (SOP) Policies & Procedure Manuals Bureaucratic Goal-oriented decision-making Competent Management Teams Competent operators Formal functional structure ('organising principle')	Foundation
3	Capability Management	Continuous Improvement (CI) Service Level Agreements (SLA) Management toolkits Project Management Systems Data-driven decision-making Risk-taking encouraged Participative style Competent Teams	HR Agenda
4	Strategic (Culture) Management	'Integrated Business Strategy' Environments screened and monitored 'High Performance Culture' 'Open' System Empowered Leadership Systemic decision-making Self Managed Teams Flexible 'Bamboo' Structure ('organising principle') 'Responsible Autonomy'	Integrated People Strategy

Organisational Effectiveness

Introduction

In chapter 2 we defined Organisational Effectiveness (OE) as:

> *Creating Roles, Structures, Processes and Practices; and*

> *Managing the Processes of Change;*
> *– To enable core business processes, and*
> *– To deploy business strategy.*

> *Building and Maintaining Employee Role Clarity and Job Significance*

In this chapter we will combine this definition with the organisational maturity levels. We then explain the HR activities, products, plans and projects that would be appropriate for each level.

The challenge for OE can be illustrated thus: "Every organised human activity... gives rise to two fundamental and opposing requirements: the division of labour into various tasks to be performed; and the coordination of those tasks to accomplish the activity. The structure of an organisation can be defined simply as the total of the ways in which its labour is divided into distinct tasks and then its coordination achieved among those tasks" (Mintzberg, 1989, p.100-101).

Level 1: Initial

Given the nature of the business at this maturity level, HR tends to offer few Organisational Design & Development (OD) solutions. Most activities and advice are basic and tactical. There will be little in the way of an organising principle to guide structure. Structure may even be designed around people and their capabilities, especially around the idiosyncrasies of the 'heroic' leaders. Most HR advice will be related to compliance with legislative requirements or union agreements, neither of which tend to inform OE.

The process of managing change is erratic and no consistency applies from one reorganisation to another. Change is a 'done to' process. Implementation is by imposition. There may be a sense of 'death by a thousand cuts'. Employees may simply be waiting for the occasion when it is their turn to be victims of management's actions. However, there is no coherent change agenda as such, only a series of semi-random change events. Management abides by the minimal requirements of the law or of union constraints whilst pushing through any changes. Change appears to be ad hoc and a fait accompli.

As we saw in chapter 3 the organisation is characterised by 'irresponsible autonomy', the HR function may appear busy but as there are few common practices, much of this will be unproductive. There will be a sense of 'reinventing the wheel' when dealing with roles and organisational structures, business & team processes and practices.

Level 2: Foundation

HR activities again mirror the state of the business at this level. Process Management demands process design, procedures, role definitions, etc. HR will focus support on crafting these for line managers. Rules will be clearly defined and delineated, as will process discipline and adherence.

OD guidance will enforce the 'organising principle' of the functional structure. Roles will be tightly defined. Role ambiguity and conflict is eradicated where possible. As no structure resolves all coordination problems, there will be HR activity on and across the 'boundaries' to resolve the residual but inevitable conflict. To complement the functional structure, organisation charts appear at this level as an OE tool. These are not merely a means of recording the structure but are actively used to design and redesign the organisation. Inefficiencies are identified and the tool is used to manage related change events.

Job Design emerges at this level. The Job Description (JD) defines the purpose, tasks and duties of each job. Each job adds value, is coherent and unique. Thus, each job can demonstrate how it adds value to the business. The job is coherent in that it consists of a collection of tasks that fit together in a meaningful way. Finally, it is unique so it does not duplicate the content or function of any other role. Through this employees start to gain role clarity at this level of maturity.

First, the JD is a foundation tool for recruitment. It defines the duties of the role as a guide to potential candidates and as a feed into the person specification (see chapter 5). Second, it is a basis for grading the job under Rewards (see chapter 8). This tends to feed into a job evaluation process.

This dual purpose also leads to the conflict and dilemma with JDs at level two. Where a tool has more than one use, either one or other use dominates or the tool misses both targets. So, either the JD is primarily a recruitment tool, a job evaluation tool or it becomes a cumbersome and unsatisfactory attempt to fulfil both functions. Many professionals will recognise this in practice. In fact, organisations at maturity level two may oscillate in the design and usage of the JD from time to time as they struggle with this conflict.

OD work will also focus on building Competent Management Teams. Team and meeting processes are addressed in an endeavour to improve management productivity. Each meeting has: a sense of purpose; the formal agenda furthers that purpose; conduct is fashioned to encourage participation in the execution of the purpose and agenda; and all members are clear on each of their own roles in the meeting. This is captured in the meeting management mnemonic: PACER (Purpose; Agenda; Conduct; Expectations; Roles).

Change Management is now a basic disciplined process in itself. Whilst the content of each reorganisation may appear unique, management pursues a full communication and consultation protocol to ensure that justice is seen to be done. Individuals and representatives are engaged in a basic dialogue over the specific and immediate change proposals. Change is regarded as a series of one-off events at this level of maturity. However, management consider the 'how' to be just as important as the 'what' of change – the means as well as the ends.

Management thus aims to manage 'critical change events'. A critical change event is defined as:

➤ Any event or management action which is (or will be) perceived to threaten the security, status, prosperity or valued working conditions of a group of employees.

Management uses suitable change tools to steer the organisation and its employees through such events. Where there is a proposal to change some critical aspect of the organisation in less than 90 days time, management draws up and tables a 'Specific Proposal' (SP). To manage a critical change event with care and sensitivity, a suitable control document is constructed to ensure all relevant managers understand their roles and their scripts – this control document is a 'Communications Pack'. The content of such a pack will differ according to the type of change event, the local conditions and the local detail of the actual specific change event. As a communication tool, the art at this level is to explain the 'local (detailed) what' and the 'how' of the change. The Communications Pack is designed to capture all the details of the Social Plan and to manage the change messages.

Level 3: HR Agenda

Functional (or vertical) clarity was established at level 2. Hierarchical or horizontal clarity is established at level 3. Accountability levels are defined and a 'flat' structure achieved. A higher level in management is not merely there to supervise the next level below; it adds value in a unique way to the overall structure. Thus, each manager is now clearly held accountable for their unique work area, core management responsibilities and accountabilities that are unique to their hierarchical level.

The core management responsibilities cover the essential tasks and skills of any manager of people. These are set out in Table 4: management at all hierarchical levels is always accountable for these generic tasks.

Table 4 Core Management Responsibilities

Core Task	Components	Accountability
Staffing		To staff the department to meets the workload demands in order to deliver the desired outcomes effectively in terms of cost, quality, time and output
	Resourcing	To recruit, select and appoint the 'right' person for each position within the budgeted headcount or establishment for the department and in accordance with the person specification
	Attendance Management	To ensure maximum attendance of employees in the department for the hours required and to manage exceptions to full attendance
Workload Allocation		To allocate the workload amongst employees in an effective and efficient manner to meet the desired outcomes, in a way that balances skills, effort, physical and mental demands, time, safety, welfare, etc.
Performance Management		To set delivery expectations and maintain performance standards & conduct in a way that creates an environment in which each employee can succeed, so that targets and schedules are met
Development		To equip each employee with the knowledge and skills to fulfil their process tasks to the required standards
	Sourcing Training	To identify and source training and development tools, courses and interventions to raise the capability of the team and individual employees
	Coaching	To enhance the capability and reinforce prior training of individual employees through 1-2-1 guidance
Communica-tions		To impart information concisely and succinctly
	Briefings	To conduct briefing sessions to the team so that employees are up to date with information on relevant policies, procedures, practices and performance
	Presentations	To convince or inform an audience on a specific topic through a formal presentation
	Meeting Management	To plan and run a meeting

Table 4 cont.

Core Task	Components	Accountability
Employee Relations		To develop and maintain a positive employee relations atmosphere
	Management by Walking About (MBWA)	To see and be seen To keep in touch
	Grievances	To deal with concerns and complaint from employees in a fair and equitable manner
	Change Management	The (micro) management of the planned change of any of the above elements

However, simply being accountable for 'supervising supervisors' does not define a unique managerial accountability. In Table 5 we define the unique accountabilities for the seven generic hierarchical levels of work. These strongly relate to Decision Making Accountabilities (Dive, 2004). The example roles are drawn from a manufacturing business.

There are in essence only seven possible accountability levels. In small organisations, levels 4-6 (or even 3-6) may actually be covered by one person. However, if there are more than seven levels in the hierarchy (which may arise due to sheer size or possibly geographical spread), accountabilities are likely to be blurred due to overlaps.

OD work will support the identification of accountability levels and the consequential changes to organisational roles and structures. The precision in role design established at maturity level 2 now moves to a higher stage of sophistication, especially due to the clarity over hierarchical accountabilities. The structure thus can be rendered 'flat'.

Jobs now evolve into roles. Jobs are static and have clear boundaries.

Table 5 Levels of Management Accountability

Management Level	Example Role	Accountability	Time Horizon
6	Global CEO	To deliver value through developing the configuration of the global portfolio of businesses and assets	7-10 years
5	Group Managing Director, EMEA	To deliver the annual and strategic plans through integrating a network or group of separate (level 4) companies and developing the 'opportunity space'*,e.g. market entry or withdrawal	Up to 7 years
4	Managing Director, UK	To deliver the annual and strategic plans for a standalone business in the specific 'opportunity space'* through optimising the allocation of resources and through targeted innovations	Up to 5 years
3	Manufacturing Director, UK	To establish, maintain and develop the infrastructures in order to deliver the annual and strategic plan	Up to 3 years
2	Factory Manager	To develop the capability of current processes and infrastructures through integrating different functional activities	Up to 2 years
1	First Line Manager	To ensure task delivery through a team of level 0 workers and through 'flexing' the work schedules	Schedule horizon of no more than 12 months
0	Production Worker	To deliver products or services to the prescribed specification	Task cycle of no more than 3 months

* 'opportunity space' is the territory, technology or product that an operating business is assigned, e.g. a national market for car production and sales. It specifies the boundaries of 'what business are we in' (WBAWI) and what business the organisation is not in.

Roles are dynamic and develop. So guidance will be needed in the direction of role development for each key player in the business. The organisation has now identified how each role contributes to the overall success of the business – there is good role-organisation alignment. This facilitates further delegation of authority. Thus, each role adds value, is coherent and unique (see maturity level 2) but is now also purposeful. That is, the incumbent can see how the role contributes to the higher purpose of the organisation. Job significance is thus enhanced.

Precision over role design can be improved by utilising full 'Role, Responsibility, Authority and Accountability' (RRAA) checklist set out in Table 6.

The RRAA statement is primarily a performance management tool and so more purposeful in its function than a JD. Whilst the RRAA may still 'feed' recruitment and rewards, it informs above all the PMS pillar (see chapter 7). This is in line with the organisational focus of level three. The detailed measurement possible at level three and the emphasis on continuous improvement demands tools that clearly define the accountabilities of each role. From accountabilities can be derived measurements (KPIs) that inform targets and thus make possible an

Table 6   Role, Responsibility, Accountability and Authority
(RRAA) Checklist

1	What does the occupant of the role do (activities/tasks)?
2	For each task, what specifically does the business hold the occupant accountable for?
3	For each accountability, to what extent does the occupant have the authority to deliver that accountability, without referral to or permission from others?
3.1	If the match between accountability and authority is less than 70%, then redefine accountability, or
3.2	Sanction greater authority (return to 2 or 3 above)
4	Finally, given all of the above, what is the coherent and consistent purpose of the role (responsibility)?

accurate assessment of actual delivery. In fact, the JD is effectively now a 'role description', as the 'narrow job' is left behind at level two.

OD activity also supports the establishment of Competent Work Teams and the use of management toolkits in decision-making processes. Meeting and team processes will change to support the new participative style and data-driven decision-making.

HR actively identifies the areas of conflict and ambiguity that lie between the different functions in the structure – the so-called 'white space' between organisational units on the organisation charts (Rummler and Brache, 1995). Liaison devices are designed and implemented to manage these residual issues. Examples of such devices include (Mintzberg, 1989, p.105):

1. Liaison roles: unique roles that act as 'go-betweens' between the respective parties

2. Inter-departmental meetings: permanent or temporary

3. Task forces: these are temporary short-term multi-functional teams assigned a particular problem to resolve

4. Project teams: a variation on the above but usually more long-term. An individual could be a member of more than one project team. The core membership tends to be permanent (unlike in a task force)

5. Integration Managers: appointed at the 'interface' of the structure, e.g. product managers in a departmental structure

6. Formal co-ordination systems: these 'build in' the

coordination and automate it, e.g. a computer-assisted integrated planning process or a common accounting system.

Change is now perceived as a continuous process of transition curves occasionally punctuated by events. Each change event initiates a separate transition curve which is in itself consciously managed (Hayes, 2002, p. 144-158). Each phase of the transition curve is also managed including the recovery phase which has its own deliberate action plan – the Recovery Plan (RP). Change is thus not simply the implementation of a new structure, for instance, but a planned transition designed to improve performance (post change event) in terms of quality, cost, time and/or output by way of a new system, structure, staffing, methodology or configuration of the organisation. An example transition curve change plan is set out in Table 7.

Table 7 Management of the Phases of the Transition Curve

Transition Phase	Facilitation for Transition Phase
Shock	Prior preparation for change Communications Pack Consultation and involvement in prior decision making and planning Communications is formal and ritualistic The announcement follows a strict structure: introduction; background; proposal; next steps Consultation but no dialogue (as this draws predictable anger) Allow time away from the work area for the message to sink in
Denial	Conflict is handled through formal consultation A personal copy of the announcement is issued Update communications on a regular basis, even where there is 'no news' Repeat the change messages Keep to the timetable Take early action to demonstrate the new reality Overt denials should be challenges but in a supportive manner Concentrate efforts on delivering the 'day job'

Table 7 cont.

Transition Phase	Facilitation for Transition Phase
Depression	Consultation agreed or exhausted Support from a third party for those exiting Support for extreme cases of depression Acknowledge feelings Informal communications focused on listening Provide space to grieve Provide further information about the new reality Help identify options and benefits Recovery plan to be agreed by the relevant management in detail
Acceptance	Remove symbols of the past Mark the endings with respectful rituals Formal communications focus on the benefits of the new future Performance targets set as challenging but achievable Highlight deadlines Bring the best from the past forward to the future, but lose the rest Let people take souvenirs and mementoes
Testing	Formal communications focused on listening, e.g. focus groups Recovery planning and actions undertaken by management – small new beginnings, e.g. small investments, new messages via new communication channels, training Provide space and time to test the new Promote creative thinking Encourage experimentation Avoid punishing mistakes Mentoring Praise success Provide feedback
Consolidation	Formal communication focused on dialogue and engagement to explore how to benefit from the new future, e.g. joint working parties Review performance and learning Recognise and reward performance Get people to help each other Broadcast successes
Internalisation	Implement new working arrangements arising from joint working parties Review change process and apply new learning for the future Conduct post-implementation reviews

Management are now more proactive in communicating and consulting over change. A longer-term perspective is taken and the company communicates its medium-term intent. Rather than simply advising staff about immediate change proposals, the organisation consults upon firm possibilities for the next 6-15 months for each group of staff. The communication messages now include the 'big what' as well as the 'local (detailed) what' and the 'how'. When the organisation is about to make an irrevocable public commitment to act, it now moves beyond announcing a Specific Proposal (SP) and makes an earlier 'Statement of Intent' (SOI). This is the confirmation of the intent to change some critical aspect of the organisation in the future. The proposed 'end game' is firm and the broad impact on employee groups is clear, but timescales and details have yet to be confirmed. This would be followed later, when the fine detail is clear, by a SP.

Level 4: Integrated People Strategy

As the business establishes 'Strategic Management', HR will demonstrate a contribution to the overall integrated strategy. The distinction between functional strategies becomes blurred and a separate HR strategy, as with other functional strategies, is less identifiable. HR supports the business in establishing environmental scanning mechanisms to constantly inform the strategy so ensuring it remains relevant and successful. Such scanning does not just include the external environment but also the internal. Hence the organisation actively canvasses the shifting views, opinions and morale of its employees (see chapter 6). Structure will constantly evolve to adapt to the internal and external pressures the business faces. HR ensures that any structural changes are appropriate and not just knee-jerk reactions; thus avoiding permanent solutions to temporary problems. Regular OE reviews take place to ensure roles and structures remain relevant and add value. A 'bamboo' structure evolves (see chapter 3).

HR contributes to the development of the cultural 'vision and values'. HR may act as the 'cultural guardian' or 'organisational conscience' to help others shift their behaviours towards the espoused values. Related OE work endeavours to instil the vision and values into all aspects of organisational life and work. The flexible structure and the 'vision and values' element emergent at this level demand a wider range of Organisational Design tools and techniques (see Stanford (2007) for a range of example techniques).

Processes are established that enable Self-Managed Teams to operate effectively. Authority levels are reviewed and delegation is pushed down to the appropriate levels in the organisation. Team and meeting processes adapt to support collegiate involvement. Decision processes are created to enable the strategy to guide judgements at all levels – systemic decision-making. Autonomy is regularly reviewed to ensure it is maximised but remains 'responsible'.

Once again, as we move into level four, a transformation occurs. At this level of maturity, personal development becomes a dominant theme (see chapter 9). With an atmosphere of 'responsible autonomy' and guided by the strategic competencies, the JD becomes a 'competency statement'. No longer only about tasks, duties and accountabilities (although these still exist), the JD becomes a Role Profile (RP): "a role describes the part played by people in meeting their objectives by working competently and flexibly within the context of the organisation's objectives, structure and processes" (Armstrong, 2003, p.198). Hence, the RP describes not just the key result areas (KRA) but also the behavioural competencies of 'how' the occupant of the role will meet those KRAs (p.198-199). In fact, it is only at this level of maturity that this addition of competencies really makes sense. For, at this level the 'vision and values' of the organisation are fully understood and accepted by employees. Employees are given the autonomy to contribute towards the organisation's aims because and only because they are aligned with the 'vision and values'. They can be trusted provided and because they demonstrate the strategic competencies (see chapter 5).

The organisation has a stronger sense of partnership with its employees when managing change. Strategy, in a broad sense, is communicated and consulted upon. The future implications of strategy for staff are open to debate. Change is part of the 'day job' – in essence 'there are no ends, only means'. Change is more of a strategic intent and continuous process rather than an event. Hence the change messages now not only include the 'big what', the 'local (detailed) what', the 'how', but now include the explicit 'why' – that is, the overall strategic imperative to change. This imperative is clearly informed by the external monitoring characteristic of this level (see Table 3).

Where the organisation intends to enter into the public domain with possible actions for the future, it makes a 'Statement of Future Intent' (SOFI). This is a declaration of the intent to change some critical aspect of the organisation in the distant future. The proposed 'end game' may be clear but timescales and details are as yet indeterminate. As details and timescales become clearer, subsequent SOI and SP are made. This completes the broad range of change management tools; a summary is set out in Table 8.

Summary

OE is about ensuring that the strange modern creation, the large organisation, actually works. HR are experts in the design of structures and processes to enable 'management through organisation'. This may be at a micro-level, e.g. meeting processes and practices, or at the macro-

Table 8 Change Management Tools

Change Event	Definition	Core Message	Definition
Public Domain Action	The organisation's intentions enter or are about to be put into the public domain	Statement of Future Intent (SOFI)	The declaration of the intent to change some critical aspect of the organisation in the distant future. The proposed 'end game' may be clear but timescales, detail and the specific impact on employee groups may still be indeterminate or dependant on external factors
Public Commitment Action	The organisation's intentions lead to an irrevocable public commitment	Statement of Intent (SOI)	The confirmation of the intent to change the critical aspect of the organisation in the future. The proposed 'end game' is now firm and the broad impact on employee groups is now clearer, but timescales and detail have yet to be confirmed
Reorganisation Action	Specific changes are proposed in no less than 90 days*	Specific Proposal (SP)	The proposal to change some critical aspect of the organisation in no less than 90 days*. The 'end game', timescales and impact on employee groups are detailed
Post-Change Actions	The consolidation following a critical change event	Recovery Process (RP)	The process of recovering from any one of the above events so as to bring performance to at least the level achieved prior to the change events

* 90 days is selected based upon the current British legal consultation period for more than 99 redundancies. An actual proposed change may take place further into the future, but is still planned and known in detail. The timing of any core message announcement should be linked to the triggering event and as soon as the detail on timescales and impact is firm.

level, e.g. the design of the total organisational structure. As the business moves through different levels of maturity, the OD activities most suitable to each level adapt. Change is managed in an ever more sophisticated manner.

A summary of the OE activities is set out in Table 9.

Table 9

	Organisational Maturity Level	HR Maturity Level	Organisational Effectiveness
1	Compliance Management	Initial	No Systematic OD activities Erratic Change Management 'Irresponsible autonomy'
2	Process Management	Foundation	Formal Functional Structure ('organising principle') Organisation Charts Job Design Job Descriptions Meeting Management Tools Basic Change Management (SP) Communications Pack
3	Capability Management	HR Agenda	'Flat' Structures Accountability Levels Role, Responsibility, Accountability and Authority (RRAA) Job Design Role Description Competent Teams supported Liaison Devices Intermediate Change Management (SOI)
4	Strategic (Culture) Management	Integrated People Strategy	'Vision and Values' in use Flexible 'Bamboo' Structure OD Tools Self-Management Teams supported Role Profiles Advanced Change Management (SOFI) 'Responsible autonomy'

CHAPTER 5

Calibre & Talent

Introduction

In chapter 2 we defined Calibre & Talent (C&T) as:

➤ *Attracting and retaining the workforce; and*

➤ *Offering Employee Career Opportunities and Progression.*

➤ *Creating a Critical Mass of Performance Enablers and Change Agents;*
  – To deliver business plans and results.

C&T is a fundamental competency of HR. It is about getting 'the right people in the right place at the right time, over time'. It is focused on populating the organisation with employees and leaders. The practices, tools and techniques used to do this vary in style and sophistication depending upon the maturity level of the organisation. As these practices develop, they offer employees increasing career prospects.

Level 1: Initial

At the initial level of maturity there is an ad hoc approach to recruitment. As vacancies arise, the wheel is reinvented, again. HR or line managers use any approach that seems relevant at the time. This may depend upon the whim of the line manager or of the HR Adviser. Thus selection is itself a random process. This is almost guaranteed as unstructured interviewing is virtually the only technique used at this level. Resourcing and selection amount to no more than 'hiring hands' and getting 'bums on seats'.

Selection often follows the unconscious principle of 'jobs for the boys'. Managers claim that they 'know what good looks like' and select accordingly. Like thus tends to attract like. Halo effects, other biases and discriminations are common at this level. If any objective basis for selection is used, it is not sustainable or persistent enough to count as a work practice. This sporadic approach to recruitment may lead to high turnover, especially for employees with relatively low service (Curtis et al, 2002, p.12-13). It is difficult for the organisation to hold onto talent (p.18).

The leaders that are sought and found at this maturity level are of the 'hero' type. As heroic effort is required to achieve virtually anything at this level, it follows that this model is self-fulfilling and self-generating. Role models arise that reinforce this image, which in turn can lock the organisation in at this level for years, if not for managerial generations. Senior 'heroes' seek to identify and develop junior 'heroes', who in turn attempt to emulate their seniors. Other leadership 'types' are either side-lined or they self-select and leave the organisation. Such hero-types tend to be performance drivers and 'hill takers', oblivious to the 'collateral damage' caused by their leadership actions.

Level 2: Foundation

This maturity level is characterised by a systematic approach to staffing and resourcing. In fact, at the Foundation level, of all the pillars of the HR Framework, recruitment has the greatest effect on enhancing the overall performance of the organisation (Curtis et al, 2002, p.31). To move the performance of the business forward necessitates 'buying in' the critical talent for the task, role and function. Hence, to gain critical leverage on company performance, HR tends to concentrate on 'top talent for top jobs' at this maturity level. As we saw in the previous chapter, when studying Organisational Effectiveness, the Job Description is a tool commonly associated with this level. To complement this in C&T, the Person Specification is a key instrument at this level of maturity. Person Specifications set out the skills, experience and characteristics of the desired candidate for any particular role. Selection processes are designed objectively to identify and appoint the 'best fit' candidate for the role. Thus the structured interview emerges at this level.

We have seen how this level of maturity is characterised by process discipline and adherence (see chapter 3). In line with this, the recruitment and internal placement procedures is symbolised by the arrival of the Personnel Requisition Form (PRF) or equivalent control document.

Having attracted recruits, the organisation also seeks to secure the effective productivity of its workforce. It manages attendance in a rigorous but fair manner. Attendance is measured and monitored through Time & Attendance Systems. Regular absentees are invited to Return to Work (RTW) interviews. Persistent absentees may be processed ultimately through the discipline procedure (see chapter 7).

As functional expertise is key to organisational performance and development at this level, a Calibre Agenda is created. The Calibre Agenda drives Calibre Acquisition, Retention, Development and Exit (CARDE). At the Foundation level the focus is on acquisition and exit. This weight of emphasis can be captured in the mnemonic CArdE.

Further, at this level the organisation identifies and attends to Critical Calibre Roles. These are roles that are expected to give maximum leverage on organisational performance. The occupants of such roles are generally assessed at least once a year. Such assessments are often 'closed' if not clandestine at this level of maturity. As the assessment is confined to critical calibre roles, this assessment exercise is ordinarily limited to senior managerial and senior technical roles. Senior players are assessed according to their perceived contribution to the organisation, and their potential for the future. In Tables 10 and 11 is a scheme for calibre classification that has been found to be robust across a number of organisations.

Table 10   Calibre – Potential Ratings

Rating	Definition
A	Consistently demonstrates the potential and competence for *step-change* progression within or outside present function
B	Has potential and competence for more progression within or outside present function and level
C	Reached own level of competence. Competent, or capable of becoming competent, at current level
D	No potential demonstrated. Demonstrates lack of competence at current level. Progressed beyond own level of competence

Step-change progression is defined as progress by two promotional levels or more

Table 11   Calibre – Contribution Ratings

Rating	Definition
5	Performs well beyond the requirements of the role. Contribution exceeds expectations
4	Sometimes performs beyond the requirements of the role. Contribution occasionally exceeds expectations
3	Performance meets the requirements of the role. Contributes as expected
2	Performance meets some of the requirements of the role, but not all. Contributes adequately
1	Consistent failure to contribute - does not meet the requirements of the role

The combination of 'Potential' and 'Contribution' describes a Calibre Profile Matrix, an example of which is set out in Table 12.

'Foundational Calibre' is the backbone of the organisation. Most standard people management practices (performance management, rewards,

Table 12   Calibre Profile Matrix

		Potential			
		A	B	C	D
Contribution	5	'Rising Stars'		'Foundational Calibre'	
	4				
	3				
	2	'Calibre Enigmas'		'Performance Problems'	'Calibre Problems'
	1				

Table 13 Calibre Actions

Calibre Category	Possible Actions
'Rising Stars'	Salary Tracking Tailored Individual Development Actions (IDA)
'Calibre Enigmas'	Career Counselling
'Calibre Foundation'	Standard Organisational Processes meet most needs
'Calibre Problems'	Performance Counselling Reassignments Calibre Exits as 'casualties of change'
'Calibre Gaps'	Seedcorn Recruitment

development) will meet the needs of this population.

For the other categories of 'calibre', bespoke actions will be required (see Table 13). Salary Tracking ensures that high calibre receive a competitive salary and package so they are not vulnerable to poaching. Individual Development Actions (IDA) are tailored actions designed to make the calibre employee feel valued by the organisation. A calibre exit is a facilitated dismissal from the business. Seedcorn recruitment is targeted recruitment to meet a critical calibre gap which cannot be fulfilled internally.

Level 3: HR Agenda

C&T takes a step-change from level 2 to level 3. The key enhancement at this level is the identification and description of a comprehensive Competency Framework. This remains however strongly functional in nature.

Job families are defined along functional lines. However, the competency levels are set such that career ladders are clear for all employees. A career ladder is a map that describes how an employee can move up the hierarchy by acquiring defined competencies. The Competency Framework allows more precision in assessing calibre but also enables objective succession planning. Succession planning allows the organisation to map out potential internal candidates for senior and critical calibre roles for time horizons from immediate replacement through to three year successors. Succession planning is greatly facilitated by the clearer levels in the hierarchy derived from the accountability levels under OE (see Table 5).

The drafting of a Competency Framework also enables the organisation to describe what its ideal leadership profile may look like. It can consciously define the leadership model it is trying to create in its talent pool. Thus, the Calibre Agenda is now enhanced by adding change agency measures, often referred to as leadership measures. These supplement the measurement

Table 14 Calibre – Leadership Ratings

	Rating	Definition
L	*'Pioneer'*	Leads others in identifying and implementing sustainable *step-change* initiatives in line with the business 'big picture'. A *pioneer* and change agent. Inspires others to change
I	*'Improver'*	Contributes ideas and suggestions effectively to *step-change* initiatives. Implements and actively supports change
M	*'Implementer'*	Effective at carrying out change initiatives primarily designed by others, often in a task leadership role. Sees such change through to completion. Tends to await the call from others
F	*'Follower'*	Prefers the status quo. Co-operates with initiatives when prompted. Neutral on change as such
B	*'Preserver'*	Actively preserves the 'way we do things'. Prevents or blocks change, actively or covertly. Holds the business back

of contribution and potential introduced at level 2. A set of leadership measures is set out in Table 14.

Given the clarity over career ladders and succession plans, the organisation is able to 'contract' with the individuals that it has identified as 'high calibre' through the Calibre Agenda. Individual Career Plans (ICP) for the highly talented are crafted. In addition, calibre gaps are identified through the succession planning process. Calibre gaps are where current or future talent needs cannot be met from internal resources. Again, 'seedcorn recruitment' will be a solution to filling such gaps, and this action is pursued by the business.

Career development emerges as a feature of this maturity level. However, it is founded upon the clear practice and career development formula: $C = f (3P, O)$. Career Development is a function of: acceptable Performance in the current role; demonstrated competency Potential for the next move; Preparation by the individual and by the organisation for that move; and a suitable Opportunity arising. This formula also guides career discussions.

Recruitment and selection shifts to a higher level of sophistication. The development of a Competency Framework enables the utilisation of techniques such as Competency-Based Interviewing (CBI), psychometric tests, and simulation exercises. These tools are used in a professional and disciplined manner. This is often backed up by research supporting the validity of their use within the organisation. Hence, full use of assessment centres sits most appropriately first at this maturity level.

Level 4: Integrated People Strategy

The organisation now goes beyond just measuring calibre at the top level and engages in Integrated Workforce Planning. It identifies the current and future workforce needs essential to meeting its strategic intent. These plans are crafted for all functions and areas of the business. These strategic needs are defined in strategic competency terms.

The organisation identifies from its integrated strategy and its 'vision and values' which competencies are most critical to its current and future success. It captures this analysis in a 'Strategic Competency Framework'. This modifies the Calibre Agenda which feeds the Integrated Workforce Plan. C&T now shifts its focus to all employees at all levels of the organisation. Calibre plans are drawn up taking into account the current and future strategic needs of the organisation.

The organisational structure is also informed by the Strategic Competency Framework. Competencies that can be outsourced are identified. Those that are core to the unique offering of the business are retained in-house.

Labour turnover is actively managed to ensure that the organisation neither stagnates nor haemorrhages. Calibre opportunities are created to allow movement. A Talent List is created and promoted. Those individuals who are considered critical for current and future calibre needs are actively promoted or assigned. Opportunities are identified or created for them. CARDE thus shifts its emphasis from acquisition and exit at level 2 to retention and development at level 4 (hence, CaRDe).

As talent is regarded not simply as a senior issue, all employees participate in an ICP as part and parcel of their personal development. This links with activities under Employee Development, which we will study in chapter nine.

Summary

C&T is the art and science of getting 'the right people in the right place at the right time, over time' – simple but deceptive. The actual activities vary tremendously across the four levels of maturity. The foundation is systematic staffing and recruitment at level 2. This is *the* HR activity at level 2. However, as an organisation 'moves through' to higher levels, the broader Calibre Agenda, informed by ever more sophisticated competency frameworks and assessments, becomes more critical to business success. As one senior executive told us "There is only calibre".

A summary of the range of C&T activities is shown in Table 15.

Table 15

	Organisational Maturity Level	HR Maturity Level	Calibre & Talent
1	Compliance Management	Initial	Ad hoc resourcing Unstructured interviews 'Hiring hands' 'Bums on seats' Hero model of leadership
2	Process Management	Foundation	Systematic staffing and resourcing Person Specifications Structured interviews Personnel Requisition Form (PRF) Attendance Management Time & Attendance Systems Return to Work (RTW) interviews 'closed' Calibre Agenda Critical Calibre Roles CArdE
3	Capability Management	HR Agenda	Functional Competency Framework Succession Planning Career Ladders Leadership Model Individual Career Plans (ICP) for 'top calibre' $C = f (3P,O)$ Career Development Competency-Based tools, e.g. CBI Psychometric Assessments Assessment Centres
4	Strategic (Culture) Management	Integrated HR Strategy	Integrated Workforce Planning Strategic Competency Framework 'open' Calibre Agenda CaRDe ICPs for all employees

CHAPTER 6

Employee Engagement

Introduction

In chapter two we defined Employee Engagement (EE) as:

➤ *Generating 'Share of Mind' for Business Messages;*
  – To inform, influence and align mutual opinions and behaviours.

➤ *Enabling Employee Voice; and*

➤ *Building Employee Involvement and Participation.*

EE is concerned with communications and involvement. In this chapter we will see how relevant HR practices progress from one maturity level to another.

Level 1: Initial

Communication at this level of maturity is spasmodic. There may be a lot of communications between managers, but precious little between managers and employees. This amount of internal 'traffic' (and noise) often fools managers into believing that they communicate a lot, and well. A feeling of 'everyone knows' arises as the managerial communication traffic gives a false sense of activity in this area of HR. However, even the managerial communication is of low quality and leads to little valuable action or change of mind.

Where employee communication does take place, it is minimal, primarily restricted to legal compliance. This may be 'imposed' on management by statute, e.g. redundancy consultation, or through the presence of strong trade unions. Thus consultation and negotiation may substitute for quality communications and for other forms of indirect employee voice. Where there are unions, employee voice is totally dependant upon internal lay union officials and practices, often at the local branch level. These are readily subject to the mood swings of 'popular democracy' and also to the 'iron laws of oligarchy': where few participate in collective behaviour, a handful of activists may exert overwhelming influence (Michels, 1968). Other than minimal compliance to statutory requirements for Information & Consultation (I&C), there is no apparent 'listening' or 'employee voice'.

As practices and procedures are fragmented across the organisation at this maturity level, disputes and grievances readily arise due to insecurity, uncertainty and inequity. Such grievances are handled in an ad hoc manner. Even if basic dispute and grievance procedures exist, they tend to be ignored or bypassed. This may be because the procedures are moribund or because they are seen as irrelevant by the local parties concerned. Thus, local deals are done regardless of the precedents this may cause for the future or for other parts of the organisation. Hence, the organisation can become locked into a series of never-ending disputes.

Where unions are recognised, the level of disputes and grievance, coupled with management style and inconsistent practices engenders an atmosphere of low trust. This locks the organisation into a continuous employee relations conflict pattern (Purcell, 1981, p.65-85). Uneasy truces may break out, but management actions are constantly open to challenge. Bargaining may be fragmented and issues are escalated quickly through the levels of procedures that are often ill-defined or just ignored.

Level 2: Foundation

The most fundamental EE activity that HR establishes at this maturity level is the effective management meeting. We examined the format of a disciplined management meeting in chapter four as part of our discussion on Organisational Effectiveness. If management cannot hold regular disciplined meetings as functional teams, then level 2 cannot be maintained in any part of the HR Maturity Matrix. The basics of good meeting management are thus essential for this level in EE. This is critical to enhancing management productivity and effectiveness, especially at the senior level where the functional structure comes together and is held together. Effective management meetings then form the basis of fundamental communications to all other employees in each function.

However, at this level the management meetings tend to be local in nature. There is no overall governance of all the management meetings across the organisation. Thus, messages are either 'big business messages' or 'small local messages'. The two are not readily connected at this level.

The management discipline associated with the local management meeting feeds basic communication channels of the 'tell & sell' or 'push' variety. Classic channels such as notice boards, newsletters, etc. fit at this level. These may be electronic in nature, but they are still basic communication techniques of low media richness. Richness is defined as the capacity of a communication medium to change understanding (Jablin et al, 1987, p.152-154).

Communication at this level consists of the 'events and newsletters' type. In both cases these are 'push' channels in that management messages are often forcibly or theatrically presented to a relatively passive audience of employees. Voice and feedback are minimal.

The conference emerges here, often for sales staff or senior managers. A lot of effort may go into such events but they still remain moderate in richness at best. The newsletter thus remains the backbone of regular organisational communications at this maturity level.

Work instructions are issued due to the process discipline characteristic of this level of maturity. In some cases these involve direct contact between employee and supervisor. However, in most modern contexts such instructions are via a works management or Enterprise Resource Planning (ERP) system. Direct instructions tend to be confrontational, whereas the anonymity of an ERP system takes the heat out of work instructions.

Other basic communication channels apparent at this level are the grievance and disputes procedures. These are clearly documented and are tailored to the structure of the organisation and the composition of the workforce. Also, they function and are seen to function in a just and fair manner. Procedural justice is seen to be done. Substantive justice is not fully realised until level 4. Where a union is recognised, formal contact through agreed procedures occurs. On a more regular basis, informal contact takes place involving both line and HR management at local levels.

Higher maturity levels in EE cannot be attained without the organisation addressing 'work ecology' issues. These are the basic health, safety & welfare issues in work. If employees' essential health and welfare are not looked after then any attempt to engage employees will be a waste of energy, and may even exacerbate the situation rather than improve it. Hence, to help address welfare issues, Employee Assistance Programmes (EAP) are strongly relevant to this level of maturity.

Where unions are recognised, there are very formal procedures that are rigidly adhered to. Bargaining is extensive and regular. However, the range of issues allowed by the procedure is limited.

Level 3: HR Agenda

There is a clear shift from 'tell & sell' at level 2 to a 'listen' mode at maturity level 3 under EE. Whilst there is still an organisational message to transmit to employees, there are new channels added at this level to enable employee voice.

At level 3, the organisation has moved on to a strong measurement basis of management (see chapter 7). This quantitative approach informs the functional messages with clear performance data for individuals, teams, groups and functions as a whole. This measurement forms the basis of the 'functional message' that management regularly conveys to employees. As we will discuss under Performance Management Systems, this data is often visual and of a short-interval nature. This data is gathered usually at the work team level, collated at the intermediate level and studied at the senior level. Ironically it is then cascaded from top functional team meetings through to work teams 'at the coalface' on a weekly or even daily basis. Shift start up meetings or 'morning prayers' will be evident where work teams assemble prior to the start of work to be briefed on performance to date and the tasks for the day. The message is, however, still strongly functional.

This cascade process becomes feasible at this maturity level for a number of reasons. First, the greater clarity of hierarchical accountability (see chapter 4) at maturity level 3 ensures value is added at each level in the hierarchy and gives each organisational level a clear sense of purpose, especially here in the communication chain. Thus the 'local' management meeting established at level 2 now fits more logically into the greater whole. With the strong functional orientation at this maturity level, a (functional) Meetings Calendar is built. Second, the abundance of KPIs provides ample material to feed a communication cascade process. The lack of such data at lower maturity levels starves regular communication channels of material. Third, because these KPIs form a sophisticated network of measures (see chapter 7) the (operational) Balanced Scorecard emerges. This tool demands a rigorous timetable of reporting to ensure the Balanced Scorecard is delivered on time. This timetable now acts as a discipline for *all* management meetings in the organisation. Thus, on the back of this, a cascade communication process is feasible. This forms the backbone of the Annual (functional) Communications Calendar which emerges as a fully effective management tool at maturity level 3. This Calendar captures all the communication events, processes and activities the organisation commits to for the full year.

The short-interval measurements (see chapter 7) offer material that sustains such communication channels as team briefings. Classic agendas for such briefings include the '4 Ps': performance; progress; policies; and people. Performance is fed by the Key Performance Indicators (KPI); and progress is fed by the Continuous Improvement (CI) agenda characteristic of this maturity level.

In addition, the 'top team' will regularly update senior executives at quarterly briefings, for instance. These are designed to keep executives who are not part of the senior team, but are key to driving business performance, informed of critical business issues. This also enables these executives to cascade any core messages to their own functions and areas.

At level 3, indirect involvement techniques come into their own. Focus groups may become evident. These are used to tap into opinion on specific topics on an occasional basis. Usually an independent and neutral facilitator leads such sessions. Variations on the Focus Group, such as 'Director Forums', may be used. Here a Director acts as the facilitator. These have often been used where the organisation has launched a specific initiative and the 'top team' wishes to engage with employee opinion directly and to 'tap into the culture'.

Indirect voice will also be institutionalised through Works Councils or other consultation bodies. This may or may not include union representation, depending upon whether there is formal recognition or unions have relevant legal rights. Such Works Councils have a broad agenda and are proactively consulted on matters of mutual interest. Engagement is on a formal basis covered by a detailed written constitution. If a union is recognised, there is extensive union participation and advanced consultation. Even in multi-union environments, there is a single-table approach. The range of agenda items covered is extensive, on a formal and informal basis.

OE Design (see chapter 4) allows the 'narrow' jobs of level 2 to develop into roles at level 3 through CI and the functional competency sets. This thus feeds direct involvement for employees through job enlargement.

Other direct involvement techniques that support the focus on CI at this level include Suggestion Schemes. The opportunities for idea generation is open due to the close measurements and the evolution of roles.

Level 4: Integrated People Strategy

At level 4, EE matures into a full 'engage' mode. Direct involvement is evident as a strategic instrument of the organisation.

The business actively indulges in direct involvement techniques such as job enrichment. Individual employees have regular 1-2-1 sessions with their line managers. Employees are also directly engaged in influencing decisions that affect their immediate work, e.g. work planning, job tasks, assignment rotation, holidays, performance targets, training & development.

In addition to all the communication techniques of lower maturity levels, the organisation is now able to convey a strong integrated strategic message. This enables an internal marketing or an 'employer branding' approach to be taken up. This feeds business messages in a broad range of channels previously not associated with communications, e.g. recruitment, induction, training, rewards, etc.

The full range of communication channels is now open to the organisation. It is thus better able to match the message to the channel. The greater the need for immediate feedback and the greater the mutual uncertainty, the greater the need for media richness in the channel(s). A range of communication techniques is set out in Table 16 illustrating the degree of 'richness' of each channel.

The business is now systematically organised through an Annual (Organisational) Meetings Calendar. What started as a local discipline at level 2 with the effective management meeting is now a comprehensive discipline across the entire organisation. This now enables the previously functional calendar to evolve into a (Organisational) Communications Calendar.

Table 16 Communication Channel Richness

Media Richness	Channel
High	Face-to-face 1-2-1s
	Workshops
	Seminars
	Director Forums
	Focus Groups
Medium	Team briefings
	Personalised Statements
	Helplines
	'Guidance' literature
	Conferences
	Online literature
Low	Emails
	Surveys
	Videos
	Newsletters
	Direct Mail
	Posters
	Notice boards

Indirect employee voice still remains relevant at this level, but is now informed more readily by the strategic approach of the business. Given the corporate strategy, and especially given the 'vision and values' (see chapter 4), the business can more readily monitor opinion and morale in a quantitative manner. Hence, opinion surveys are most relevant at this

Table 17 Employee Engagement Generic Agenda Items

The economic and financial situation
Investments
Employment patterns and manning levels
Organisational changes
Collective redundancies
New working methods and productivity initiatives
Health, safety and welfare arrangements
Training
Transfer of undertakings
Rates of pay
Terms & conditions
Promotional and transfer arrangements
Procedural arrangements
Working hours, holidays and rosters
Overtime working and arrangements
Work allocation
Job design

maturity level. Until the business acquired a comprehensive integrated approach, any survey would tend to be a wide trawl of random views. The 'values' guide which opinions to seek out and how.

Employee voice, such as through Works Councils, is more able to hold to agenda items of a strategic and long-term nature as other practices deal with more domestic issues. Hence, shift briefings now evolve into 'Quality

Circles' etc. which seek to resolve local but also cross-functional problems. The degree of employee involvement in EE channels is dependant upon the agenda items and degree of authority actually delegated. A comprehensive range of agenda items is set out in Table 17.

Under an employee relations heading, at this level of maturity, management and unions enter intro a true state of partnership. Long-term consultation on plans and performance take place. A high level of trust exists between representatives and contact is on a regular and often on an informal basis.

Summary

In this chapter we have described the communication and involvement practices relevant to each level of maturity. The progression in the quality and sophistication of engagement activity and techniques is evident as the organisation attains higher maturity levels. More importantly, the implied cultural shift is also clear. Employees are not 'engaged' at level one as they are a mere resource; at level four they are strategic assets and partners.

A summary of the EE practices is given in Table 18.

Table 18

	Organisational Maturity Level	HR Maturity Level	Employee Engagement
1	Compliance Management	Initial	Poor communications ('noise') No listening Legal and collective compliance Information & Consultation (I&C) – statutory consultation only Union negotiations if forced Continuous Employee Relations (ER) Conflict Pattern Disputes and grievances over insecurity and inequity No or restricted employee voice
2	Process Management	Foundation	Effective local management meetings 'Big' business messages and 'small' local messages 'Push' and 'send' communications channels Basic channels: notice boards 'Event and newsletters' Conferences Work instructions Health, Safety & Welfare actively addressed Employee Assistance Programme (EAP) Grievance, etc. procedures Consultation Procedure Procedural justice Traditional Formal Trade Union Bargaining Local union engagement (if recognised) "Tell & Sell"
3	Capability Management	HR Agenda	Functional 'message' Director Forums Top Team Briefings HR 'Breakfast' meetings Shift 'morning prayers' Monthly (cascade) team briefings (Functional) Management Meetings Calendar Annual (functional) Communications Calendar The '4 Ps' Briefing Agenda Employee Surveys Suggestion Schemes Indirect (functional) Employee Voice Focus Groups Extensive Union Participation Works Councils Job Enlargement "Listen"

Table 18 cont.

	Organisational Maturity Level	HR Maturity Level	Employee Engagement
4	Strategic (Culture) Management	Integrated HR Strategy	Internal Marketing Employer Branding Strategic business messages 'Strategic' Opinion Surveys Direct involvement (Organisational) Management Meeting Calendar Annual (organisational) Communications Calendar 1-2-1s for all Job Enrichment 'Quality Circles' Procedural and Substantive Justice (ER/TU) Partnership "Dialogue"

Performance Management Systems

Introduction

Previously we have defined Performance Management Systems (PMS) as:

➤ *Deploying Business Strategy and Aligning Personal Performance.*

➤ *Creating an Environment in which each Employee can Succeed.*

In chapter two we outlined the focus of PMS. It is concerned with the range of systems directly or indirectly designed to channel and encourage employee behaviour to concentrate on the interests of the organisation and its dominant stakeholders. As PMS techniques evolve through the four maturity levels we will also see how well they facilitate employee success. In order to meet the conditions of this definition, we would seem to need a strategy. However, as should now be apparent, a fully integrated strategy is only explicit at maturity level four. At best, organisational strategy below this level will be 'emergent' (Mintzberg, 1989, p.29-34). That is, the strategy will be the accumulation of all the actions and activities of organisational players. We will thus see how the PMS adapt in order to meet the definition's conditions, as the organisation moves through the different maturity levels.

Level 1: Initial

At this level, the exclusive measure of performance, in any formal sense, is budget delivery. This may be measured on an annual, quarterly or monthly cycle. It is rarely measured at intervals of more than one year. In fact, most budgets are reset at least annually and may be referred to as Annual Operating Plans (AOP). However, these are rarely plans as such but simply financial forecasts or commitments. The content of the budget may vary according to the nature of the organisation. In a commercial setting the budgets will measure profit, cost, revenue and possibly net cashflow. However, the prime measure is profit or operating income. The PMS is embedded in, and limited by, the financial reporting system. Hence, performance management below the cost centre level and outside of financial control systems is effectively absent.

Other responsibilities or accountabilities are not measured on a systematic basis, other than when they 'go wrong'. This reflects 'compliance' which is characteristic of this level of organisational maturity. However, from time to time, other delivery concerns do arise in the organisation. These ad hoc requirements arise due to the limitations of financial controls and targets. Finances are incapable on their own of offering sufficient control and monitoring of a large organisation. Separate reporting may be demanded to monitor such initiatives, but they rarely connect to the rest of the PMS. Consequently, there are a lot of legacy reports generated long after the temporary requirements of the original initiative have expired. As the PMS does not integrate these initiatives, they tend not to be sustainable. They require special effort to monitor, and hence systematic management of them is difficult to maintain.

Individual performance management is measured on an ad hoc basis. This also tends to be on a negative basis with minimal if any feedback. Rewards do not line up with performance. To the question "Am I doing OK?" the answer is likely to be "Well, you are still here, aren't you?!?"

Rudimentary disciplinary action, formal or informal, arises at this level. However, as there is no systematic management of individual performance, low level, early counselling and disciplinary action does not take place. Thus, performance problems 'suddenly' arise. Performance may 'suddenly' be deemed unacceptable and the individual summarily dealt with. Dismissal may be the only means of managing poor performance. As even at this level, dismissal is still an extreme act, under-performance is tolerated by neglect and by a lack of decent monitoring and measurement systems. However, the lack of self-monitoring also means that the underperforming individual is unlikely to be aware of their shortcomings.

Level 2: Foundation

At this maturity level, through Organisational Effectiveness (see chapter 4), job design creates focused 'narrow' jobs. This facilitates the clear definition of jobs & duties throughout at least the management population. This focus enables an Annual Appraisal System to work, alongside other PMS such as the budgetary reporting systems. It is at this level we would expect the classical system, Management by Objectives (MbO) to appear and sustain.

SMART Goals are set annually and formally recorded. SMART Goals vary in definition, but below is a common set:

1.   Specific – precisely defined

2.   Measurable – quantitatively

3.   Achievable

4.   Relevant – to the role and to the aims of the organisation

5.   Time trackable – progress can be monitored on a regular basis.

These goals may be divided into categories such as financial, project and personal. However, they are almost exclusively functional in scope. Occasionally there are company-wide initiatives that are intended to persist from year to year, e.g. safety. These may be incorporated into personal goals.

Mid-year reviews are held to reappraise the relevance of the SMART goals, to evaluate progress and to correct goals to reflect changes in duties and circumstances beyond the control of the individual. At the end of the year a full year review is conducted and recorded. The results may feed through to pay review processes (see chapter 8).

PMS at this maturity level may be reserved for senior executives and members of management teams. Budget holders and those deemed to have a significant influence over business and functional decisions and performance are included in the goal-setting and review processes. At this level, PMS is not built into the regular routines of the operation so appraisals are seen as 'bolt-on' events with a twice-yearly cycle.

For sales staff, PMS will be evident, often on a monthly basis, through Sales Incentive Plans (SIP). Three to five specific sales measure are targeted, usually derived from the AOP. Measures may include net sales, gross margin, net margin, cash collected through accounts receivable, new sales wins, etc. The SIP is then linked to sales incentives (see chapter 8).

Formal performance improvement procedures are evident at this level. Where performance persistently falls below the expected level, a formal Performance Improvement Planning (PIP) process is instigated. The line manager discusses the problem with the individual and an agreed plan is crafted. Through coaching and counselling, or other suitable support, performance is raised. Poor performance is managed first through raising awareness, second through performance counselling and then third through the formal disciplinary procedure proper. Failure to meet the expected standards results in disciplinary action and ultimately in dismissal.

Level 3: HR Agenda

The precision and frequency of PMS shifts up a gear at level 3. This level is characterised by a multitude of short-interval measurements for functional processes as well as functional results. At this level we see the emergence of systematic functional KPIs – Key Performance Indicators. These track and measure factors that have been identified as critical to the effective and efficient management of key business processes and desired business outcomes. Such KPIs are measured on an hourly/daily/weekly basis, as appropriate. The frequency is dependant upon the criticality of the KPI and the corrective action cycle time. If a process can go critical in two hours and the corrective action time is 30 minutes; as a control, there is little value in measuring the KPI on only a daily basis. Targets & Measures (T&M) are evident throughout the organisation and for every function.

Continuous Improvement (CI) targets are set and projects commissioned to enhance the performance of key business processes and activities. Thus capability is not only managed, it is constantly enhanced. CI projects are measured in terms of on time, in full (OTIF) to the agreed milestone plans. The expected delivery from projects is also measured through systematic Project Benefit Tracking.

At this level, the range of KPIs is captured in a Balanced Scorecard or equivalent system (Kaplan and Norton, 1992). This provides a 'dashboard' of measures designed to guide the business decision-making processes. However, at this maturity level the dashboard is more of a collection of important functional measures rather than a set derived from a clear and coherent business strategy. It is thus an operational Balanced Scorecard.

Operational KPIs are apparent throughout the organisation. These are used to monitor and guide performance in key areas. KPIs are most evident through Visual Management. The organisation uses a range of communication devices that tell "... at a glance how work should be done and whether it deviates from the standard" (Liker, 2004, p.152).

A closed-loop performance cycle is manifest, based upon the 'management by exception' principle (Wren, 1994, p.115). Only when a measure is out of tolerance or off-target does it enter this cycle. Then a Variance to Target (VTT) is registered. This leads to a Root Cause Analysis (RCA) to identify the underlying reasons for the adverse variance. This leads in turn to the specification and agreement of appropriate Corrective Action (CA) to bring the measure back on track. Following the CA, a Measure of Effectiveness (MoE) of the CA and the original performance is appraised. The checklist set out in Table 19 summarises the closed-loop performance cycle.

We saw when discussing Organisational Effectiveness (see chapter 4) how the role accountabilities at this maturity level can be more precisely captured

Table 19 Closed-Loop Performance Cycle

1	Variance to target (VTT)	On plan (OTIF percentage)? On target?
2	Root-cause analysis (RCA)	What are the root-causes of any adverse variance? Who is accountable for the root-causes?
3	Corrective action (CA)	What action can the person accountable take to bring the measure back on plan and/or on target? If the RCA suggests that the CA needs to be carried out under a different accountability, what action can the relevant person take to bring the measure back on target and/or plan?
4	Measure of Effectiveness (MoE)	Was the person accountable effective in delivering the accountability? Was any CA effective in bringing the accountability back on plan and/or on target?

in a Role, Responsibility, Authority and Accountability (RRAA) Statement. This OE tool now feeds a PMS tool – the Individual Accountability Review (IAR). The analysis in the RRAA enables individuals to have their accountabilities more precisely defined. The flat structure and the accountability levels permit such precision. To craft an IAR the process below is followed:

1. Restate the accountabilities of the role from the RRAA Statement

2. For each accountability, how is delivery *measured*?
   2.1 If no clear direct measurement is available, identify a surrogate measure, or
   2.2 If no measure is available then redefine the accountability more precisely (return to 1 above)

3. For each measurement(s), what *targets* for the hour/day/week/month/quarter/year will contribute to the achievement of the business strategy?

4.   To deliver each target, what projects will be needed?
   4.1   Hence what *milestone plans* will be needed to track the progress of the project?

The IAR then enables a more defined evaluation of performance. The individual's performance may then be captured on an Individual Contribution Report (ICR). A model for an ICR is set out in Table 20. This can record monthly and quarterly performance which can then roll up into an ongoing as well as an annual review.

At maturity level 3, the PMS becomes part of the organisation's DNA. It becomes a fully integrated routine for management, on a regular short-interval basis. Formal recording then takes place for reward or sanction purposes at set intervals. Often this recording is done at a quarterly

Table 20   Individual Contribution Report

Name:	Role:
Date:	
Accountability:	*What precisely are you held accountable for?*
Target for Quarter/Year	*What targets are set/agreed?*
Milestone Plan	*What plans, if executed, will help you hit the targets?*
Actual Result	*What was actually achieved (in the quarter/year)?*
Variance	*Is the plan and target on track or adverse in this review period?*
Root-Cause	*Why is the plan or target adverse?*
Corrective Action	*What will you do to bring the plan and/or target back on track?*
Review	*When will you/we review this corrective action and how?*
Effectiveness	*How effective was your original performance and any corrective action?*

frequency. Hence, the performance evaluation does not come as a surprise to manager or individual. There is a climate of 'management by consequence': rewards and sanctions clearly follow from the level and quality of performance delivery.

The PIP process that emerged at level 2 evolves into a more sophisticated scheme at level 3. The PIP process at level 2 tends to assume that 'one size fits all'. However, sub-standard performance and conduct (short of gross misconduct) is not uniform. Marginally sub-standard performance warrants a completely different approach (and associated conversation) to seriously sub-standard conduct. Hence, for example, a 'CRAGS' model now guides managers in how to approach such situations, and what kind of discussion to enter into with the relevant employee. The more serious the shortfall in performance, the more accelerated the management reaction. A 'CRAGS' Model is set out in Table 21.

However, as the focus of this level of maturity is continuous improvement, the aim of any PIP is first and foremost to return to acceptable employee performance as quickly as possible. Thus, the organisation invests to turning round underperformers, even if this entails redeployment to a more suitable role or organisational level. The assumption of the 'amber' track in the 'CRAGS' Model is that the employee's performance can be turned around. It is only in the more critical tracks of 'red' and 'crimson' that urgent action is needed to prevent a dismissal.

All of the tools and practices outlined in this section support the theme that runs throughout this maturity level – 'Expectations Management'. The close measurement of processes, targets, CI, etc. are all designed to communicate clearly to the employee the behaviours that are expected of him. To further set such expectations, management may specify in some detail the Minimum Standards of Performance (MSOP) in terms of inputs, processes and outputs for each role.

Table 21 'CRAGS' Performance Model

Code	Performance Category	Definition	Example	Management Action
S	'Silver'	Employee's performance significantly exceeds expectations, targets and/or standards	110% or more of sales target	Feedback Praise Over-target bonus scheme
G	'Green'	Employee's performance meets expectations, targets and/or standards	100-109% of sales targets	Thanks Continue to monitor
A	'Amber'	Employee's performance falls marginally below expectations, targets and/or standards	90-99% of sales target	Support Agree Corrective Action
R	'Red'	Employee's performance falls significantly below expectations, targets and/or standards	80-90% of sales target	Raise concern and awareness Formal PIP If no improvement – disciplinary action
C	'Crimson'	Employee's performance falls seriously below expectations, targets and/or standards	Below 80% of sales target	Raise alarm Warning Critical PIP Fast-track discipline action

Level 4: Integrated People Strategy

The integrated business strategy converts the PMS at this maturity level. The strategy allows the previously functional KPIs to transform into true Strategic KPIs (SKPIs). The organisation is now able to define its 'dashboard' by which it can navigate and drive its strategic performance and capability. Here the 'dashboard' introduced at maturity level 3 transforms into a true *strategic* Balanced Scorecard.

These SKPIs are systematically cascaded throughout the organisation, transforming functional, team and individual T&Ms. Strategic projects are defined and also incorporated into the PMS, again measured by On Time in Full (OTIF) to the agreed milestone plans. Sophisticated monitoring processes keep all these T&Ms under constant review. The T&Ms are informed by functional external benchmarking to set 'best in class' aspirations and ambitions for teams and individuals.

T&Ms are further enhanced by 360° 'goal-setting'. As the organisational structure has now evolved into a flexible model, possibly matrix, the hierarchical style of PMS (which is characteristic of lower maturity levels), is no longer sufficient. 'Internal customers' now input to the target-setting process (Machin, 1980). The mutual expectations of internal customers and suppliers are discussed and defined. These are all then captured in the PMS.

Individuals have regular 1-2-1 reviews with their managers, ordinarily on a monthly basis. Performance is reviewed and coaching given. Root Cause Analyses (RCA) are discussed and Corrective Actions (CA) agreed. In essence, performance reviews reduce to one simple question, "Are we 'On Time, In Full' to the agreed (strategic) milestone plans?"

The introduction of the Strategic Competency Framework further enhances the PMS. As the competencies are deemed critical to the future success of the organisation, they are tracked, measured and reported in the PMS.

The whole PMS is now an integrated system: real-time data, real-time targets and real-time feedback through an automatic measurement system. This allows regular self-monitoring of process and target performance to be conducted as part of the comprehensive Visual Management System first introduced at level 3.

Summary

PMS is core to organisational success. If the organisation cannot assure that actions lead to intended outcomes, then it is doomed. This chapter has demonstrated how this core control mechanism progresses from one level of maturity to another. From the 'bolt on' appraisal at level two, to the fully integrated real-time, self-monitoring PMS at level four, the organisation progressively monitors and guides behaviours.

A summary of the HR activities in PMS is set out in Table 22.

Table 22

	Organisational Maturity Level	HR Maturity Level	Performance Management Systems
1	Compliance Management	Initial	AOP/Budget Delivery No formal systematic feedback mechanism Ad hoc reports Dismissal as only rectification tool
2	Process Management	Foundation	Clear definitions of Jobs & Duties Focused (narrow) 'jobs' Management by Objectives (MbO) SMART Goals Annual Appraisals Mid-Year Reviews Full-Year Reviews Sales Incentive Plans (SIP) Performance Improvement Planning (PIP) process Discipline Procedure
3	Capability Management	HR Agenda	'Expectations Management' 'Management by Consequence' Functional KPIs Operational Balanced Scorecard(s) Short-interval measurements Team and individual T&Ms Continuous Improvement (CI) plans and targets Project Benefit Tracking Visual Management Individual Accountability Reviews (IAR) Individual Contribution Report (ICR) Daily/Weekly/Monthly/Quarterly Reviews Closed-loop performance cycle: VTT ⇨ RCA ⇨ CA ⇨ MoE Minimum Standards of Performance (MSOP) 'CRAGS' PIP

4	Strategic (Culture) Management	Integrated People Strategy	Shared strategic direction cascaded
			Strategic Balanced Scorecard
			Deployment of strategic KPIs
			Aligned and cascaded individual and team T&Ms
			External benchmarking ('best in class')
			360° target-setting
			Strategic Competency Performance Measurement
			Automated Measurement Systems:
			    • Real-time data
			    • Real-time targets
			    • Real-time feedback

Rewards & Recognition

Introduction

Previously we defined Employee Rewards & Recognition (R&R) as:

➤ *Creating the 'Message in the Money'; and*

➤ *Maintaining a 'Good' Standard of Living; and*

➤ *Being Competitive in the Chosen Market(s);*
  – To align motivation with strategic intent.

➤ *Attaining 'Just' Recognition and Desserts.*

The managerial aim of R&R is the historical aspiration of all employers, since time immemorial: to get employees to do their bidding, willingly. We will see how the implicit and eventually the explicit reward model of the organisation evolves as it steps through the four different maturity levels. We will also see how successfully employees may fulfil their aims in terms of R&R.

Level 1: Initial

The focus of R&R at this maturity level is (unconsciously) exclusively on extrinsic motivation. The underlying assumption is that money will solve all problems and that all employees are 'in it' for the money.

However, there is no unified reward structure. The realised structure is either inherited, is traditional in nature, or is simply the accumulation of past practices with no guiding principles. In practical terms, reward packages may well be unique to each individual. This leads to a sense of inequity, feelings of relative deprivation and resentment. Formal and informal grievances arise because individuals doing the same job are rewarded differently. There is no rhyme or reason to explain the current reward structure or the differences in individual packages.

Where rewards are reviewed and enhanced, through salary rises and/or bonus payments, there is no congruence in practice and hence the 'message in the money' is confused. Money is a message to employees, however crude, and at this maturity level the message is perplexing. Bonuses especially will be used to reward heroes and heroic action. Action heroes are prized and encouraged.

The only coherent system at this level is payroll administration. The prime reason for payroll being systematic is, however, financial control and tax compliance not employee motivation.

Level 2: Foundation

In all other pillars of the HR Maturity Matrix, a functional approach is established at level 2. However, R&R is different. At maturity level 2 a unified company-wide reward structure is established. Without such a company-wide approach, grievances will remain due to differential practices and consequential inequities. A sense of parity across the whole company is established and maintained making higher maturity levels possible and to support other pillars of the HR Framework (Curtis et al, 2002, p.32).

Parity is established and maintained both horizontally and vertically. Horizontally, all jobs of a similar 'size' are placed on the same reward packages. Vertically, jobs of a larger 'size' are put onto packages of a proportionately larger range. This necessitates the introduction of a number of HR tools.

First, from the functional structure (see OE in chapter 4 and C&T in chapter 5), job families are identified. Roles are then evaluated from top to bottom and a grading structure is created. Roles are benchmarked with the chosen labour markets to inform the grading structure and also to craft a Terms & Conditions (T&C) Matrix. This matrix sets out the different terms & conditions that apply at the different grades: salary bands; on-target bonus rates; car allowances; private medical insurance; notice periods; eligibility for overtime or flexitime; etc. Benchmarking enables 'external' parity to be established and maintained.

At level 2, the reward structure becomes highly standardised, if not bureaucratic. Grades, salary bands and authorisation levels restrict the discretion of local managers from making pay rises. This limits their ability to reward individual contributions (Curtis et al, 2002, p. 162). This heavy standardisation counters the relative chaos of level 1. The lack of short-interval individual performance management at level 2 makes senior management reluctant to grant more power to lower levels of management.

The organisation communicates reward packages in a partial manner to its employees through a handbook or a more comprehensive employee portfolio. An employee portfolio is the individual's repository for all the documentation that defines the relationship between the employer and the employee. This includes a contract of employment, relevant policies and procedures, company literature such as its history and purpose, etc.

'At risk' earnings apply to two groups at this level – managers and sales staff. Managers are eligible for Short Term Incentive Plans (STIP). The design of these may appear complex or simple depending upon the messages that the organisation wishes to send to the relevant group of staff. However, at this level all management bonus schemes tend to be variations on profit-share schemes. Even where there is apparently a portion linked to personal goals, this tends to amount to only a small percentage of total target cash.

We saw in chapter 7 that sales staff are commonly subject to a detailed PMS through Sales Incentive Plans (SIP). These focus on a narrow range of sales measures, usually 3-5 in total. These targets are then linked to a Sales Incentive Bonus (SIB). The scheme is crafted on a 'hard formula' basis, i.e. given the actual value of the sales achieved versus targets, the SIB can be readily calculated. Payment may be on a monthly basis, but the limited sophistication of measurement systems at level 2 tends to force payment on a less frequent basis, e.g. quarterly or annually.

In line with the formal bureaucracy of this maturity level, a Payroll Change Form (or equivalent control document) ensures that any changes to salary or other terms & conditions has due authority. The criteria for adjusting compensation are clearly prescribed in policy statements (p.200). All changes to payments need formal justification.

For most staff though, rewards remain an annual event. Where there are recognised trade unions, some rewards may be subject to negotiation.

Level 3: HR Agenda

At maturity level 3, the organisation has built up sufficient experience and confidence to make its reward structure transparent and more readily understandable. This openness enhances the sense of fairness individuals expect of a reward structure. The business will thus publish its reward structure so employees can comprehend the policies and principles underlying the reward practices.

The organisation also reforms its rewards to ensure unique reward product positioning. Just as a company's product positioning should enable it to make one unique offering in each of its chosen market segments, so a reward manager positions each reward product. For instance, it is not uncommon for performance to be rewarded by both salary rises and bonus payments. This is inefficient and also confusing for internal players. The organisation at this maturity level will, then, reposition salary and bonuses such that, for example, salary becomes linked to calibre (see chapter 5) and bonus linked to short-term individual performance (see chapter 7).

In chapter five we saw that the Calibre Agenda targets high calibre individuals at level 3. To complement this approach, R&R allows for differential reward practices to support the Calibre Agenda. For instance, whilst the business may have a pay policy that benchmarks salaries with the median in the chosen labour market, the R&R Strategy may add a calibre premium. Calibre individuals may then be benchmarked against the upper quartile of the chosen market. This then gives scope for attracting high calibre candidates for key roles and retaining them once on board. This introduces the element of 'personal equity' for a few employees. This will be covered more generally at maturity level 4 below.

As we saw under Performance Management Systems (see chapter 7), at maturity level 3, individual contribution to the greater whole is much more evident. Through defined accountabilities and close measurements, the individual's contribution to the overall organisation is apparent. To complement this, management bonus schemes shift from a profit-share scheme to one focused on individual contribution. Overall funding of the STIP Scheme may still be linked to profit; the actual distribution of such funds to each eligible individual is, however, then based upon personal contribution.

The expansion of jobs into roles that is encouraged at this maturity level provides scope for employee discretionary effort. Thus, recognition schemes are more likely to emerge and thrive at this level. Such schemes provide one-off awards for 'going the extra mile'.

The company moves on from employee portfolios to Total Reward Statements. Here the organisation gives each individual an annual valuation of their full package. Many employees take compensation & benefits for granted and are oblivious to the true value and potential advantage of the overall package. Part of transparency is to open employees' eyes to this reality.

Level 4: Integrated People Strategy

Salary is now not just linked to performance but also takes into account strategic competencies introduced under C&T (see chapter 5). As these competencies are seen as enhancing the potential for the organisation's future, pay is regarded as an investment in that future. Thus, the reward model moves from Performance-Related Pay to Contribution-Related Pay (CRP) (Armstrong, 2003, p.700-704).

On the reward side, all employees now participate in Profit-Related Pay bonuses. All enjoy the fruits of collective success. Choice is further extended by 'flexible benefits'. This widens the benefits open to employees, whilst allowing each employee to tailor their package to suit their individual and family circumstances.

Overall though, at this maturity level pay is treated as a hygiene factor rather than a motivator per se. Thus management's driving force is to build and maintain reward equity: horizontal, vertical, external and personal. Horizontal, vertical and external are echoes of the parity principle introduced at level 2. Personal equity relates to the subjective sentiment on the part of the individual as to how well rewarded and motivated they feel in terms of 'what they bring to the party'.

As cash rewards are now positioned as hygiene factors, the organisation moves to broader reward and recognition practices. Management demonstrates its appreciation of employee effort through vehicles beyond salary and bonus: awards, one-off gifts, time off and other recognition techniques are widely utilised.

Summary

Motivation and money are closely associated in the world of work. In this chapter we have seen how more sophisticated approaches develop as the organisation and HR move through the maturity levels. At lower levels of maturity, money tends to dominate. However, whilst money is always on the agenda, an interest in broader reward factors progressively emerges at higher levels. Motivation as a systematic and conscious 'tool', however, only fully appears at level 4. Here the organisation systematically examines what makes its people 'tick'. Further, it seeks to model the 'motivational deals' or psychological contracts which trigger desired behaviours. We shall explore motivation more fully in chapter 9.

Table 23

	Organisational Maturity Level	HR Maturity Level	Reward & Recognition
1	Compliance Management	Initial	Extrinsic Motivation 'Money solves all problems' No unified reward structure Confused 'messages in the money' Bonuses for 'heroics' Basic Payroll Administration
2	Process Management	Foundation	Company-wide unified Reward Structure Vertical, horizontal and external 'parity' Job Families Grading Structure Market benchmarking Terms & Conditions Matrix Short Term Incentive Payment (STIP) for management: profit-related Employee Portfolio including Contract of Employment 'Hard formula' Sales Incentive Bonuses (SIB) Payroll Change Form Rewards as an annual event
3	Capability Management	HR Agenda	Comprehensible and Transparent Reward Structure Reward product positioning Calibre-Differentiated Rewards Performance-Related Pay (PRP) STIP: individual performance-related Recognition Schemes Total Reward Statements
4	Strategic (Culture) Management	Integrated People Strategy	Intrinsic Motivation Defined 'psychological contract(s)' Contribution-Related Pay PRP bonuses for all Flexible Benefits – 'Choice' Money as a hygiene factor Equity: Vertical; Horizontal; External; Personal

A summary of R&R is set out in Table 23.

Employee Development

Introduction

In chapter two we defined Employee Development (ED) as:

➤ *Raising People Capability in terms of knowledge, skills and process abilities.*

➤ *Establishing Personal Competence; and*

➤ *Developing Performance Excellence.*

In this chapter we will map the changing themes and techniques in ED as the organisation shifts from one maturity level to another. We will also see to what extent employees have the opportunities to develop their own competencies and then to excel in performance.

Level 1: Initial

At this level, ED, as with all other HR activities, is ad hoc. Most learn their trade by 'sitting next to Nellie': that is, simply observing another experienced operator (at whatever level in the organisation). Hence, the acquired skills are almost entirely dependant upon the quality of the tutor. Bad practices can thus persist for generations. Certainly, practice will vary according to the number of 'Nellies' and the diverse processes that they adopt on any one day of 'instruction'. Alternatively, where no such tutor exists, development is through the 'university of hard knocks' as the individual is simply 'dropped in the deep end'. This is development by the 'sink or swim' methodology.

In other respects, ED may be almost entirely absent, except when compliance with regulations demands it. ED activity is spasmodic, depending upon the bias or penchant of the General Manager. So, sudden initiatives may apparently necessitate ED, but with little analysis or rationale. Alternatively a favoured consultant may be regularly engaged to run development activities, but with no Training Needs Analysis (TNA) to justify the activity objectively.

As with other pillars of the HR Strategy Framework, some ED activities will be bestowed upon the favoured few. Junior apprentice 'heroes' will be fed excessive development support whilst others are starved of any such help.

Level 2: Foundation

ED is guided by two themes at this level of maturity: "Establishing Operational Effectiveness"; and "Developing Managerial Skills".

Process Management is the title of the organisational maturity level 2. Here business and operational processes are clearly defined and carried out in a consistent and repeatable manner. Part of assuring such conformance to standards is training for all operators (at all levels of the organisation) in the Standard Operating Procedures (SOP) relevant to their jobs: hence the theme of "Establishing Operational Effectiveness". This is one of the means of instilling and maintaining common standards of process abilities. The organisation thus develops and offers Basic Job Training (BJT) for all employees, but especially management level zero employees (see Table 5). BJT also establishes employee personal competence.

BJT is of little value however if the skills and techniques are not reinforced back at the workplace. Hence, each employee's manager is taken through an appreciation course of the very same BJT to enable them to carry out On-the-Job Reinforcement (OJR). Periodically OJR will also act as 'refresher' training for the employee.

We saw in chapter 3 that a fundamental aim at this level is to install effective management teams. Thus the organisation defines a 'core curriculum' of basic management skills and hence training. This ensures that managers are competent at delivering operational and people skills implied by each of the pillars of the HR Framework, especially at the level of first line managers (FLM). FLMs are critical for ensuring SOPs are maintained thus reinforcing process discipline and adherence. We discussed in chapter 4, when dealing with OE, the generic responsibilities of managers at all levels of the hierarchy (see Table 5). In Table 24 we set out a fuller account of the generic core curriculum for FLM training that support these responsibilities.

Some of the standard managerial procedures and practices are captured in such documentation as a Managers' Handbook. This gives guidance on all aspects of people management. This may be a hard copy and/or an online resource.

Table 24 Core Curriculum for First Line Manager Training

Core Task	Components	Knowledge	Skills
Staffing		Department and Team goals Workload levels and profile Working arrangements and contractual conditions Basic employment law	
	Resourcing	Budgeted Headcount Job Descriptions Person Specifications Competencies Recruitment Policy	Interviewing and Selection
	Attendance Management	T&A System Attendance Policy & Procedure Shift and holiday rostering	RTW Interviewing
Workload Allocation		Planning Systems Work Systems SOPs Safe Systems of Work Work Assignments Projects	Job Design Instructions Basic Project Management Delegation
Performance Management		KPIs Appraisal System Performance Environment Checklist Discipline Procedure Fair and unfair dismissal laws	Target setting Monitoring Dialogue and Feedback Appraising Investigating Discipline hearing
Development		SOPs Person Specification	
	Sourcing Training	Competencies PDP Process Training solutions available	Competency ratings Basic TNA
	Coaching		Coaching

Table 24 cont.

Core Task	Components	Knowledge	Skills
Communica-tions	Briefings		Preparing a brief Delivering messages Handling Questions
	Presentations		Presenting
	Meeting Management	PACER	Chairing
Employee Relations		Components of a positive employee relations environment Discrimination Laws	
	Management by Walking About (MBWA)		'Zooming' Influencing skills
	Grievances	Grievance Procedure	Investigation Grievance meeting
	Change Management	Planned Change Models Consultation Procedure	Consultation Skills Handling Objections

ED activities are also designed to support induction or orientation of new employees. This ensures that from the start, employees acquire the general knowledge of the company and where they fit into it. Where an employee transfers from one role to another or from one department to another, a form of internal (re-)orientation is also conducted.

All ED is fully informed by objective and rigorous Training Needs Analysis

(TNA). This makes sure that ED actions are not misguided. Whilst the optimal development solution may not eventually prove to be training, a TNA still kicks off the whole process.

Level 3: HR Agenda

At level 3, ED activities are guided by an additional theme: "Enhancing Leadership". The Competency Agenda at this level established under Calibre & Talent (see chapter 5) defines leadership qualities and characteristics. The crafting of a conscious and detailed leadership model now informs the ED Agenda. It is then the responsibility of ED to deliver programmes, tools and techniques to enhance leaders' knowledge, skills and process abilities.

The focus here is on the 'leadership group', often the top 1% of the organisational population. Each of these senior players has a Leadership Development Plan (LDP) to identify strengths and development needs against the leadership model, and to craft bespoke solutions for such needs. The LDP may be informed by results derived from development centres or from psychometric analyses.

In support of the Calibre Agenda under Calibre & Talent, ED facilitates bespoke Individual Development Plans (IDP) for those individuals identified as 'high calibre'. Such IDPs may offer a wide range of development options; the actual development solutions may merely be whatever gives the individual the feeling that the company values them.

We saw in chapter 7, when discussing Performance Management Systems, that the IAR and ICR were relevant to level 3. These are strongly devoted to performance and short-interval measurements. This has a 'crowding out' effect upon the development aspect that is often incorporated into Appraisals (introduced at level 2 under PMS). Hence, at this level of maturity a separate discussion is held with each employee to create a Personal Development Plan (PDP). This facilitates the identification of strengths and development needs, all within the context of the functional competencies (see chapter 5). PDPs are updated at least annually and development is reviewed on a regular basis by manager and individual. The separation of this process for employee development from performance management enhances the quality of the dialogue. Commonly in Appraisals, objective-setting, reviews of performance contribution *and* personal development are all lumped into one process. These multiple aims tend to confuse participants and devalue the overall procedure. The nature of the discussions for these different aims is diverse so a clearly distinct procedure aids the development aim. Career Development Training (CDT) is introduced to support the PDPs and prepare employees for their next promotion or development move in line with the career ladders associated with C&T (see chapter 5). CDT prepares employees for their next promotion or development move. In addition, Basic Job Training (BJT) is now fully informed by the functional Competency Frameworks.

As mentioned under Organisational Effectiveness (see chapter 4), management adopt a range of toolkits to advance the Continuous Improvement (CI) agenda. These toolkits may include the likes of Six Sigma, Lean Manufacturing, Triz, TQM, Taguchi methods, etc. ED supports these activities by offering suitable 'toolkit' training and related skills development. To support the theme of CI at this maturity level, the organisation creates and offers systematic project management training.

Level 4: Integrated People Strategy

ED activities at this maturity level will resemble those associated with Knowledge Management and the Learning Organisation (Senge, 1990; Armstrong, 2003, p.160 and p.533). The organisation seeks proactively to capture and utilise the intellectual property rights within its human capital. ED activities come to be driven by the additional theme of "Supporting Personal Development".

As the organisation is now guided by the Strategic Competency Framework (see chapter 5), it is in a much better position to judge the relative merits of personal development activities. It can objectively assess which personal development initiatives may progress its strategic competency agenda and which may be a distraction. Whilst it encourages all employees to develop, this is still related back to the strategic intent of the business. Thus, the PDP at this level of maturity is enhanced by the appearance of the Strategic Competency Framework over and above the functional.

As the organisation has now identified the competencies that proactively further its strategy, it is able to craft suitably supportive ED activities. Thus Performance Excellence Training (PET) is established. PET enables employees to attain higher levels of delivery in their current roles in line with the Strategic Competency Framework. This training enables the PDP to be enhanced.

Mentoring is systemically built into the development solution set for the organisation. Experts in each strategic competency are identified; a bank of related knowledge is built enabling employees to tap into this knowledge base. Role models are then on hand to coach employees. These role models are themselves trained in coaching techniques.

Staff indulge in external study tours and visits to glean new and innovative practices that may be adopted and adapted by the business.

Summary

ED and training shift emphasis as the organisation moves through the maturity levels. From the 'sink or swim' school at level one to comprehensive personal development at level four, development solutions increase in sophistication as the organisation matures. Key themes guide ED at each level, but these themes build up as we move to the higher levels.

A summary of ED is displayed in Table 25.

Table 25

	Organisational Maturity Level	HR Maturity Level	Employee Development
1	Compliance Management	Initial	Spasmodic or absent development Ad hoc training 'Sitting next to Nellie' 'Sink of Swim' ED for the favoured few
2	Process Management	Foundation	"Establishing Operational Effectiveness" "Developing Managerial Skills" Basic Job Training (BJT) On-The-Job Reinforcement (OJR) Core curriculum for First Line Managers Managers' Handbook Induction/Orientation Training Needs Analysis (TNA)
3	Capability Management	HR Agenda	"Enhancing Leadership" Leadership Development Plans (LDP) for top players (Functional) Personal Development Plans (PDP) Career Development Training (CDT) Competency-based BJT Management training Project Management Training
4	Strategic (Culture) Management	Integrated People Strategy	Knowledge Management Learning Organisation "Supporting Personal Development" Mentoring Enhanced PDP Performance Excellence Training (PET) External visits and tours

Employee Motivation

Introduction

EM is not strictly part of the HR Maturity Matrix. However, the Matrix has significant implications for EM which we will explore in this chapter.

The definition of EM is:

➤ *Creating a Motivation Framework for Employees*
  – That aligns with business and cultural aims, and
  – Both shapes and meets realistic and genuine individual expectations.

First, a cautionary note. Motivation per se cannot be managed in any meaningful or direct manner. Motivation is inherently personal and not accessible to direct management. However, the concept of the psychological contract (Armstrong, 2003, p.297-306) implies the possibility of striking such a deal. For, the organisation determines (but not consciously) which of the wide range of possible psychological contracts it may support. Such a 'contract' both shapes individual expectations and also meets pre-existing expectations. This is set in the context of the aims and limited resources of the organisation; hence such expectations need to be realistic.

EM is at the heart of the employment relationship. It is the implicit employer-employee 'deal'. It relates back to the 'two sides of HR' and the inherent conflict in HR work that we covered in chapter 2. All possible EMs are available at all maturity levels. However, as we will see, each level systematically enables certain EMs whilst other levels prove problematic at supporting some EMs. This makes the 'choice' over the nature of the psychological contract challenging for organisations. This choice is constrained by the level of maturity of the organisation at any one time.

For ease, and because the model is comprehensive, I have chosen the range of 'motivations' that are set out in Warr (2007). Where a 'motivation' is mentioned in this chapter that is derived from Warr, it is set out in italics.

Level 1: Initial

As we saw in chapter 8 when discussing R&R, organisations at this maturity level are almost exclusively focused on extrinsic motivation. *Money* is regarded as the solution to all problems. In essence, money is the only solution systematically available to management at this level. Money is seen as the main reason for coming to work. Thus, the psychological contract is primarily transactional and short-term in nature. This is reinforced by the sense of job insecurity that is felt at this level. Ambiguity tends to be high and other hygiene factors are generally neglected.

Other EMs are available but generally only for the privileged few. Job status is open to a few senior managers. There are clearly *opportunities for personal control* for senior players due to the sense of 'irresponsible autonomy' that is characteristic of this level. However, the heightened job and environmental ambiguity present for most will crowd out most chances for self-determination.

Level 2: Foundation

Several EMs become open at this maturity level.

The PMS Appraisal System provides the chance for *externally generated goals*. SMART Goals and Management by Objectives (MbO) enhance this factor. As long as such goals are: optimal (neither too high nor demanding, nor too low); the tasks are complete in nature (p.163); and there are minimal conflicts with other goals and requirements; then the goals will tend to be motivational (p.158-9).

The tightly defined jobs, the systematic use of Job Descriptions (JD) and Standard Operating Procedures (SOP) all give a degree of *role and environmental clarity* to employees, thus reducing role ambiguity and related anxiety. Three elements arise at level 2 that tend to reduce this type of anxiety (p.191): standards of required performance; work method procedures; and work sequence scheduling.

Basic Job Training (BJT) and SOPs provide the opportunity for *skill use* and the demonstration of personal competence. Success at a task leads to raised aspiration levels (p.154).

Under EE (see chapter 6), we saw that Health, Safety & Welfare was systematically addressed to manage hygiene factors. This gives an element of physical *security* to employees. In addition, through EE and R&R just procedures and reward parity give an early sense of *equity*. This is not fully available however until level 4.

Supervision at level 1 can border on the abusive. At maturity level 2, the BJT for managers and especially First Line Managers (FLM) provides a more *supportive supervisory environment* for employees.

Level 3: HR Agenda

New EMs become more readily available at level 3.

The creation of the functional Career Framework (see chapter 5) provides *career opportunities* and progression to employees. This also enhances the awareness and probability of attaining *valued social positions* within the organisation.

Task variety is provided through the shift from jobs to roles and the Continuous Improvement (CI) Agenda that emerges at this level. This is reinforced through job enlargement. Similar to goals discussed under level 2, an optimal level of *variety* would appear to be motivational (p.183-7). Too much or too little variety has a negative effect upon an individual's motivation and happiness.

Goals are further enhanced at this level through the appearance of KPIs, short-interval measurements and CI targets. A fourth element in terms of *role clarity* adds to the three mentioned in level 2: regular feedback on actual performance (p.191). The short-interval measurement enhances the opportunities for such regularity, which tends formally to be only, twice-yearly at level 2.

Level 4: Integrated People Strategy

The organisation makes the final shift to a full 'intrinsic' motivational framework at this level of maturity. We saw in chapter 4 that the business is able to articulate its 'vision and values' as part of its integrated strategy. It may even have described its ideal culture. From this, the business is able even to define the range of motivations open to individuals and consciously chooses which ones it will actively support (and which it will not support) through an EM Strategy. For instance, the company may choose to support achievement motivation but not status motivation. This then informs the range of psychological contracts that the business may proactively promote. In essence, the business addresses the question "What are the (psychological contract) 'deals' that we will support for our employees?" This strategic choice over EM then informs all the relevant activities of HR. For example, if one of the psychological contracts chosen by the business is a 'developmental' one, then Employee Development (ED) overlaps the EM Strategy.

The organisation actively seeks to enhance the Quality of Working Life (QWL) and Work-Life Balance of its employees. This is informed by evidence from employee surveys, audits and focus group feedback (see chapter 6). There is an evident enthusiasm for and activity to support personal growth.

The atmosphere of 'responsible autonomy' provides a wide scope for *personal control* at this level for most if not all employees. The greater an individual's control over her environment, the greater her happiness, up to a point. Some studies suggest that high levels of control can lead to anxiety over decision making and overload (p.149-152).

Job enrichment under EE further enhances *variety*.

The R&R Agenda progresses to allow for vertical, horizontal and now personal *equity*. At maturity level 4 both procedural (established at level 2) and now distributive justice is more assured (p.135-140).

Summary

We have seen how a comprehensive range of EMs fits alongside the HR Maturity Matrix. Whilst all EMs are available to some extent or other at all levels, the widespread relevance of each EM is determined by the maturity level of the organisation. Hence, an organisation is constrained in any 'choice' it may care to exercise over the nature of its psychological contract(s). For a level 1 organisation to pretend it offers developmental opportunities to any but the privileged few is folly. For a level 1

Table 26

	Organisational Maturity Level	HR Maturity Level	Employee Motivation
1	Compliance Management	Initial	Money Contact with Others
2	Process Management	Foundation	Externally-Generated Goals Environmental and Role Clarity Security Opportunity for Skill Use Supportive Supervision Equity (Horizontal and Vertical)
3	Capability Management	HR Agenda	Valued Social Position Variety Career Opportunity and Progression
4	Strategic (Culture) Management	Integrated HR Strategy	Opportunity for Personal Control Equity (Horizontal, Vertical and Personal)

organisation to pretend it offers great *opportunities for personal control* is also futile. Motivation is thus a dependant variable – dependant upon organisational maturity. To open up wider EMs, an organisation must develop.

A summary of EMs as derived from Warr (2007) is set out in Table 26.

The Strategic Roles of Human Resources

Introduction

In this final chapter, we pull together all of the arguments set out in the book so far. We will show how the HR Maturity Matrix can be transformed from a descriptive and analytical tool into a Strategic Plan for action. First, we will examine the various roles of HR.

The Prime Roles of Human Resources

The prime role for HR shifts as the organisation moves through the different maturity levels. Whilst to some extent there will be an element of all of the roles described below, at each maturity level, one HR role and style emerges and predominates at each level.

Maturity Level 1 – Initial

At level 1, HR as a department, may be non-existent. The organisation may see little or no value in having a separate devoted specialist department to deal with 'staff' issues. Residual administrative functions may exist, but these may be spread across a number of other departments, such as Finance. There may not be a professional HR function in its own right at all.

Where HR does exist at level 1, its prime role is that of 'fire-fighter'. As the business processes and practices at level 1 are grossly inconsistent and disputes arise due to inequities, HR will be running around dealing with each issue as a 'one-off' in a reactive manner. Quick fixes are inevitable, further exacerbating feelings of inequity. No sooner has one issue been resolved, than this sets off another grievance. As the organisation is locked into a compliance mode, HR will also act as 'police' over internal and external regulations, whether these are statutory or imposed through collective bargaining.

Ironically, HR may find itself overworked at this level. Managers displace their responsibility for people management practices to HR (Curtis et al, 2003, p.18-19). Such practices as recruitment and identifying training needs are considered 'administrative' and not 'managerial' tasks. Hence, HR staff may find themselves carrying out direct managerial tasks rather than supporting line managers in designing and executing such duties. Only when line managers take full personal ownership of people management issues can an organisation move to the next level (p.19-20).

Maturity Level 2 – Foundation

At level 2, HR shifts into a service provision mode. The services cover the traditional HR activities relevant to maturity level 2. As has been discussed, the principle contribution HR makes to business performance

116

at level 2 is through systematic staffing and recruitment (see chapter 5). Hence a core HR service will be that of resourcing. As will also be apparent from the text so far, company-wide reward management becomes a key central service at this maturity level (see chapter 8). The HR function is focused on establishing and maintaining service competency. The style of the department will be 'responsive' to client requirements and demands.

In common (and in conjunction) with the rest of the organisation, the HR department will establishes its own policies & procedures, probably captured in a manual of some sort. The exact content of this 'manual' will depend upon the demands and requirements of the organisation and the local legal framework at the time. However, it will cover at least the core fundamental processes of the HR department. A minimal set is presented in Table 27. This set effectively defines the basic professional practices of any HR department. Many of these are covered in the main text of this book so far. Without these processes being robustly defined and applied, no higher level of maturity will be possible for the HR department, and hence for the larger organisation.

Maturity Level 3 – HR Agenda

At level 3, HR as a department moves into an advisory role. Here HR is sought out as an active expert function that is regarded as genuinely adding value. Line managers are reluctant to progress without seeking out the expertise of their HR advisors. It is at this point that HR can openly articulate an overt HR Strategy. Below this maturity level, an explicit strategy would seem extravagant, misplaced or excessive. HR's performance is also measured by its own KPIs, in common with all other functions at this level. However, this strategy and the KPIs are not yet fully integrated with the rest of the organisation as 'strategy' at this maturity level is still functional in character for all departments.

Table 27 Fundamental HR Processes

HR Strategy Pillar	HR Process	Comments
Organisational Effectiveness	Job Description Design	Benchmarking
	Communications Pack	Specific Proposal
	Organisation Charts	
Calibre & Talent	Resourcing & Selection	External and internal Person Specifications Personnel Requisition Form (PRF)
	Starters Procedure	
	Leavers Procedure	
	Attendance Policy and Procedure	
Employee Engagement	Grievance Procedure	
Performance Management Systems	Discipline Procedure	
	Performance Improvement (PIP) Guidelines	
Employee Development	Basic Job Training (BJT)	
	First Line Manager (FLM) Training	Covering all basic people management skills
Reward & Recognition	Grading	Job Evaluation System and Processes
	Terms & Conditions Matrix	
	Salary and Contract Change Process	Payroll Control Form
	Contracts of Employment	
	Annual Pay Review Pack	

Maturity Level 4 – Integrated People Strategy

HR now builds on previous levels and roles and adopts the enhanced role of 'Business Partner'. As the organisational strategy is now a fully integrated one, the distinction between functional strategies becomes blurred (hence 'people' strategy not simply 'HR'). People issues are seen as central to all strategic considerations. HR is a full proactive member of each management team, from top to bottom.

The roles of HR are summarised in Table 28.

Table 28 The Roles of HR

	Organisational Maturity Level	HR Maturity Level	HR Role	HR Style
1	Compliance Management	Initial	Absent Fire-Fighters Compliance Police	Reactive
2	Process Management	Foundation	Service Providers	Responsive
3	Capability Management	HR Agenda	Advisors	Active
4	Strategic (Culture) Management	Integrated People Strategy	Business Partners	Proactive

From Change Agents to Strategic Plans

Even though an HR Strategy is only overtly relevant to maturity levels 3 and 4, this does not mean that a strategic perspective is not pertinent to all levels. At first, HR may simply choose or default to adopt the role most relevant to the identified maturity level of the organisation. This is the 'match' option. So the initial strategic questions for HR are:

1.   "What is the current Maturity Level of the organisation?"

2.   "What HR activities in each pillar of the HR Framework need to be improved to support and match the current Maturity Level of the organisation?"

The first task is always to diagnose the maturity level of the organisation as it currently presents. The descriptions in the previous chapters should enable a fairly accurate diagnosis of the current organisational and managerial practices. Also, under each one of the pillars of the HR Framework, the current state of HR and people practices should be apparent. It is worth reminding ourselves that, as with all counselling and facilitation, we can only start where the client is; hence the need to diagnose the current organisational state. By matching the HR maturity level with the organisational level, the HR function puts itself 'in pace' with and congruent to its client business.

However, HR may choose to adopt a proactive change agent role and thus go beyond the 'match' option. Such a proactive option requires HR to take on broad diagnostic, facilitation and executive skills. It is common for an organisation to remain 'stuck' at any given maturity level. Levels are in themselves strongly self-reinforcing. Further, as we have already stated, to move from one level to another requires a step-change, not a gradual evolution. As with a thermodynamic phase transition, additional energy is required to achieve such phase shifts. As a rule, an organisation cannot sustainably remain at more than two (adjacent) levels in terms of maturity (current and 'working towards'). So, logically it suggests that action should be first devoted to addressing the 'lowest' maturity level achieved to date in the HR Maturity Matrix.

The next strategic question then arises:

3.   "How will we (as HR) help the organisation to move forward
      (to the next level of maturity)?"

The organisation thus has the choice over which pillar(s) of the HR
Framework to apply energy to, and in what order. This is a strategic
choice which is informed by the demands and needs of the specific
business.

As an aside, there is a critical note of caution here: HR cannot get
significantly 'out of pace' with its client organisation without facing dire
consequences. If the organisation, for instance, is at maturity level 1, any
attempt on the part of HR to establish an HR level of, say 3 will be
doomed. If a support function like HR endeavours to outpace its clients
(or its stakeholders) by more than one step, it will fail. First, that 'higher'
level will not be sustainable in such an unconducive organisational
environment. Second, implementing HR activities of a level 3 nature in a
level 1 environment will be seen as irrelevant and extravagant by the
client organisation. This would leave the HR function and staff exposed
and vulnerable. Third, attempting to establish, for instance, the role of
business partner (level 4) when the function has yet to build service
competency associated with level 2 will undermine HR's credibility.
Without these strong foundations, the role associated with a higher level
will be seen as unsustainable and inappropriate.

By answering the change agency questions above, and by setting
priorities over the consequential answers, and taking resource constraints
into account, the following strategic question may be answered:

4.   "What is the (rolling) 3-Year Action Plan for HR?"

It is not possible to do everything at once. Further, as has been discussed
throughout this volume, it is not sustainable to operate at multiple levels

of the Maturity Matrix. Hence, given all the activities that an HR function may wish to implement, there will be a virtuous sequence which builds each pillar of the HR Plan. Thus, given the resource constraints of every HR department, and given the desired HR activities, a 3-year plan can be drawn up.

"Plan on a Page"

An HR Plan can be complex. The detailed project plans can run to many pages. This is difficult to hold in one head and hold together. That is why we have found it valuable to write the strategy as a "Plan on a Page". At a glance, this can identify priorities and guide understanding and action. An example template is given in Table 29.

This plan follows the logic of the maturity levels. For instance, until level 1 is fully rectified in all areas and under all pillars, it is inappropriate to commission actions at level 2, and so on. The strength of the HR Matrix is not only the vertical build of actions in each pillar but also the horizontal build of complementary actions across the pillars, but at the same level of maturity. Thus disparate actions isolated in a sub-specialism of HR, through the HR Matrix, are shown to be related in concept and are further reinforcing in reality.

By portraying actions as a "Plan on a Page", project timescales may be added, and the forward picture can be readily seen. By using the HR activities and organisational maturity levels in the body of this book (and captured in the summary tables at the end of each chapter), actions that are relevant to the context and needs of the specific organisation can be extracted and added to the "Plan on a Page". The numeric notation may draw on the concept of 'virtuous sequencing' so that the plan builds in a complementary and sustainable manner.

Table 29   HR "Plan on a Page"

HR "Plan on a Page"

Maturity Level	OE	C&T	EE	PMS	R&R	ED
1	Action #1 Action #2		Action #3		Action #4	Action #7
2 (Current identified organisational maturity level)		Action #5		Action #6		
3						
4						

Conclusion

In this book we have presented a *roadmap* that facilitates the navigation of HR Strategy. We have developed HR Strategy *through* HR practice. The HR Matrix is a comprehensive yet succinct tool that allows us to draw a "Plan on a Page" - to empower each and every HR professional to plan what to do next. We have placed HR Strategy within a generic organisational strategic context, that of the maturity level. Through all of this, we have successfully linked HR Strategy with HR practice. We have put strategy into practice; and practice into strategy. Thus we have bridged the gap between the rhetoric of HRM Strategy and the reality on the ground (Armstrong, 2003, p.124-5).

All organisations have a 'plan' whether they know it or not. This plan may even be accidental. Any plan needs deploying unless it is meant to remain a fantasy document for exercising the mind or for the purposes of decorative display only. In large enterprises, strategic deployment is *through* organisation. The experts in organisation are HR.

A business plan (deliberate or emergent) needs to be deployed through an organisational structure; that structure needs to be populated with the right calibre and talent; that talent needs clear direction through performance management systems; the consequential performance then needs evaluating and rewarding; and so on. The management of this sequence of processes is normally assigned to a Chief Operating Officer (COO). Yet the content is all HR. Hence, it is time that HR stepped up to the plate and took on its true role in their respective enterprises. A command of the integrated framework set out in this book can make the function truly strategic and thus put HR in the driving seat. HR will then deserve its place at the Board table.

ACRONYMS

AOP	Annual Operating Plan
BJT	Basic Job Training
BSC	Balanced Scorecard
C&T	Calibre & Talent
CA	Corrective Action
CARDE	Calibre Acquisition, Retention, Development and Exit
CBI	Competency-Based Interview
CDT	Career Development Training
CEO	Chief Executive Officer
CI	Continuous Improvement
COO	Chief Operating Officer
CRAGS	Crimson, Red, Amber, Green, Silver
CRP	Contribution-Related Pay
EAP	Employee Assistance Programme
ED	Employee Development
EE	Employee Engagement
EM	Employee Motivation
ERP	Enterprise Resource Planning
FLM	First Line Manager
H, S & W	Health, Safety & Welfare
HR	Human Resources
HRM	Human Resources Management
I&C	Information & Consultation
IAR	Individual Accountability Review

ICP	Individual Career Plan
ICR	Individual Contribution Report
IDA	Individual Development Action
JD	Job Description
KPI	Key Performance Indicator
KRA	Key Results Area
MBWA	Management by Walking About
MoE	Measure of Effectiveness
MSOP	Minimum Standards of Performance
OD	Organisational Design & Development
OE	Organisational Effectiveness
OJR	On-the-Job Reinforcement
OTIF	On Time, In Full (to the Plan)
PACER	Purpose, Agenda, Conduct, Expectations, Roles
P&P	Policies & Procedures
PDP	Personal Development Plan
PET	Performance Excellence Training
PIP	Performance Improvement Plan
PMS	Performance Management Systems
PRF	Personnel Requisition Form
PRP	Performance-Related Pay
QWL	Quality of Working Life
R&R	Rewards & Recognition
RCA	Root-Cause Analysis
RP	Role Profile
RRAA	Roles, Responsibilities, Authority and Accountabilities
RTW	Return to Work
SIB	Sales Incentive Bonus
SIP	Sales Incentive Plan
SKPI	Strategic Key Performance Indicator
SLA	Service Level Agreement
SMT	Self-Managed Team

SOFI	Statement of Future Intent
SOI	Statement of Intent
SOP	Standard Operating Procedure
SP	Specific Proposal
SSW	Safe System of Work
STIP	Short Term Incentive Payment
T&C	Terms & Conditions
T&M	Target & Measure
TNA	Training Needs Analysis
TQM	Total Quality Management
VTT	Variance to Target
WBAWI?	What Business Are We In?

BIBLIOGRAPHY

Ackroyd A and Thompson P, 1999, Organisational Misbehaviour, Sage

Armstrong M, 2003, A Handbook of Human Resource Management Practice, Kogan Page

Barrett L, Dunbar R and Lycett J, 2002, Human Evolutionary Psychology, Palgrave

Collins D, 2000, Management Fads and Buzzwords, Routledge

Curtis B, Hefley W E and Miller S A, 2002, The People Capability Maturity Model, Addison Wesley

Dive B, 2004, The Healthy Organisation, Kogan Page

Hayes J, 2002, The Theory and Practice of Change Management, Palgrave Macmillan

Jablin F M, Putnam L L, Roberts K H and Porter L W, 1987, Handbook of Organisational Communications, Sage

Kaplan R S and Norton D P, 1992, The balanced scorecard – measures that drive performance, Harvard Business Review, Jan-Feb p.71-79

Kearns P, 2010, HR Strategy: Creating Business Strategy with Human Capital, Butterworth Heinemann

Liker J K, 2004, The Toyota Way, McGraw Hill

Machin J L, 1980, The Expectations Approach, McGraw Hill

Michels R, 1968, Political Parties, The Free Press

Mintzberg H, 1989, Mintzberg on Management, Free Press

Perrow C, 1999, Normal Accidents, Princeton University Press

Purcell J, 1981, Good Industrial Relations, The Macmillan Press

Rummler GA and Bracke AP, 1995, Improving Performance: How to Manage the White Space on the Organisation Chart, Jossey-Bass

Senge P, 1990, The Fifth Discipline: the art and practice of the learning organisation, Doubleday

Sievers B, 1986, Beyond the Surrogate of Motivation, Organisation Studies, Vol. 7/4, p.335-351

Simons R, 1994, Levers of Control, Harvard Business School Press

Stanford N, 2007, Guide to Organisation Design, The Economist Press

Ulrich D, 1998, A New Mandate for Human Resources, Harvard Business Review, Jan – Feb, p.124-134

Warr P, 2007, Work, Happiness and Unhappiness, Lawrence Erlbaum Associates

Wren D A, 1994, The Evolution of Management Thought, Wiley

INDEX

.